To: Tige and Jack

Two "clutch" individuals.

Bob Sloan
1/24/19

Clutch

HOW RITUALS ELEVATE
PERFORMANCE AND HAPPINESS

Dr. Mark Powell

Copyright © 2018 by Mark Powell

Clutch: How Rituals Elevate Performance and Happiness

All rights reserved, including the right to reproduce this book or portions thereof in any form.

First edition February 2018

ISBN 978-1-943157-59-4

Design by Hillary Davis

Manufactured in the United States of America

To Stephen and Ashley
who make this dad beam.

ACKNOWLEDGMENTS

The fingerprints of amazing people
are all over this book.
The lovely Annie Powell, who celebrated
every word of every draft
and chased copious covert citations.
Editors, Laura Tokie and Jennifer Beltramo,
who shared their genius and gave me a voice.
Napa painter Gail Chandler,
who took an afternoon
to help a stranger
express effervescence in orange acrylic.

CONTENTS

Introduction		ix
Section One		**1**
1	Hot, Quick and Dangerous	3
2	Get in the Zone	11
3	The Personal Power Ritual	17
4	Who Needs to be Clutch	27
5	Start Building Your $(R + C)^n$	35
Section Two		**47**
6	Introduction to Power	49
7	The Power of Fun	55
8	The Power of Recovery	61
9	The Power of Bandwidth	67
10	The Power of the Familiar	75
11	The Power of Inspiration	79
Section Three		**85**
12	Personal Power Rituals in Action	87
13	Win the Morning – Win the Day	95

Section Four	**105**
14 Clutch Fitness Introduction	107
15 My Running Breakthrough	111
16 Your Personal Power Ritual for Running 5K	117
17 The Cadence of Regular Exercise	125
18 The Myth of Eating Habits	135
19 Deconstructing Your Old Way of Eating	141
20 Struggle and Success	149
21 Build Your Weight Loss Routine	153
22 Craft Your Weight Loss Ceremony	165
23 You Can Rise to the Occasion	173
Appendix: Ritual Power for Your Groups	*177*
References	*183*
Bibliography	*191*

INTRODUCTION

Rob is a gifted screenwriter in New York. I called him and said, "Rob, you know every movie ever made. I need your help. I'm giving a keynote address on *Clutch* and I'm looking for a movie clip. One capturing a clutch performance. Someone rising to the occasion. Maybe battling back from adversity. Overcoming odds. Can you think of any movie with a scene like that?"

Being kind, my friend didn't laugh out loud. The scene I sought is pretty much in every movie ever made. It's why we buy the ticket. We never tire of seeing someone rise to the challenge.

Jennifer Lawrence as the raw and courageous Katniss Everdeen, stepping up to save her sister and become the first volunteer from District 12 in *The Hunger Games*.

Robin Williams delivering John Keating's soaring Carpe Diem speech from on top of a desk in *Dead Poets Society*.

Emma Watson's Hermione Granger outwitting Lord Voldemort to save her friend Harry.

DR. MARK POWELL

Russell Crowe alone on the coliseum floor before the evil Emperor Commodus declaring, "My name is Maximus Decimus Meridius, commander of the Armies of the North, General of the Felix Legions and loyal servant of the true emperor, Marcus Aurelius. Father to a murdered son, husband to a murdered wife. And I will have my vengeance, in this life or the next."

Clutch places fascinating academic studies alongside stories of successful women and men who have risen to their big game challenges. The studies and stories reveal how performance and happiness are elevated by the use of ceremonial routines which we call personal power rituals.

Clutch isn't a book about famous actors, athletes and achievers. *Clutch* is a book about you. *Clutch* is a book about what you are trying to accomplish. Whether you are starting a new business or starting a new diet, entering the NFL or entering the 8th grade, opening on Broadway or opening a taco shop, *Clutch* will show you how to rise to your challenge.

Clutch

SECTION *one*

———

DR. MARK POWELL

CHAPTER *one*

HOT, QUICK AND DANGEROUS

In the Zion Canyon of southwest Utah lives the green gecko. He sports orbital eyes that see in all directions but cannot blink. He can lick his eyeballs should the need arise. The green gecko is cold-blooded.

I didn't pay close attention in Mrs. Rankin's 8th grade science class so I had to refresh myself on what exactly cold bloodedness was about. Warm-blooded animals have warm blood. Cold-blooded animals have cold blood – sometimes. Sometimes they have warm blood. Sometimes even hot blood.

The green gecko takes on the temperature of his environment. After a hard day in the canyon, when he is ready for a little hibernation, he chills in a cool crevasse. Later he awakens slowly. Very slowly. And hungry. Very hungry. He longs for the crunch of a cricket kabob.

The green gecko has a problem. He's ready to eat, not ready

to hunt. With blood flowing like autumn molasses he couldn't catch two old crickets in a potato sack race.

To hunt his dinner and avoid becoming snake bait, our lethargic lizard needs to get up to speed. He knows exactly what to do. He does it every day. Call it the green gecko hunting ritual.

First, he moves to a sundrenched hot rock. Second, he angles his body just so, like my daughter on the beach at the Jersey Shore, so as not to waste a single ray. Third, he spinnakers his ribcage for maximum surface area. Fourth, he darkens his dermis to draw even more heat.

He is transformed.

From cold, slow and vulnerable, he becomes hot, quick and dangerous.

Rising to the Occasion

Don't you love those days when you are hot, quick and dangerous? Everything comes easy. You are having fun, recovering from small setbacks with ease, feeling energized and inspired. Those A-game days where you possess accomplishment attributes. Focus. Confidence. Creativity. Clarity.

Some days, I'm not my best me. I'm off. Cold. Slow. Vulnerable. Do you share my experience? If so, here's the question. What if tomorrow you can't chance being slow, cold and vulnerable? What if tomorrow is your big game?

CLUTCH

What if...

Tomorrow
You play in the Super Bowl
Suit up for the World Series
Tee off at the Masters

Tomorrow
You argue before the Supreme Court
Sit for a final exam
Interview for the job of your dreams

Tomorrow
You open on Broadway
Audition for The Voice
Deploy with SEAL Team Six

How do you get your head on straight? How do you bring your best you to your big game?

The Problem of High Stakes Errors

Tom knows the pressure of the big game. Tom trains top law school prospects to take the Law School Admission Test. The LSAT. He has trained 1300 of the best and the brightest. He works with each student for at least six months. He brings his students to the point where if they were taking the LSAT untimed in their living rooms they'd pretty much get every answer right. Then he adds the time limitation. He then replicates a real LSAT test day by moving students to a classroom with other test takers. Students take 30-50 full practice tests leading up to game day.

When I spoke with Tom, I asked, "Let's imagine you have a top student who has taken 50 practice tests and she averages, say 176, with which she's a hop, skip and a jump into Harvard Law. Tomorrow she takes the real test. The one that counts. Her big game. Will she score a 176?"

"I'm afraid not," Tom replied, dropping his voice. "Maybe 1 out of 100 will put up their best score ever. About 7% will hold their ground. Everyone else will experience a discouraging drop of 3-7 points from their practice test averages. Unfortunately, it seems, the more it means to a student, the more they want it, the bigger the drop." High stakes errors.

A team of researchers from Caltech led by Benedetto De Martino published a study that demonstrates what Tom observed.[1] Participants were instructed to throw a ball at a target. Baseline accuracy was established. Next, those participants were offered a small cash prize for hitting the target. Guess what? With a little incentive, accuracy improved. Finally, the participants were offered a large cash prize to hit the target. This time our well-practiced, highly-motivated participants looked like they had been told to throw with their opposite hands. Coordination left the building. Throughout the study, researchers tracked brain activity using a functional MRI. When a greater prize was at stake, quite unfortunately, brain function slowed down.

Therein lies the challenge. When the stakes are highest, even people who have practiced or prepared struggle. This book offers a strategy to overcome the struggle of decreased performance in

CLUTCH

high stakes situations. Whether your dream is to be a scholar or speaker; athlete or artist; cardiologist or Kardashian - you face this challenge. How do you bring your A-game when it matters most? How do you become hot, quick and dangerous when it counts? When you find yourself in base camp of your own personal Everest, how do you harness all of your talent, experience, strength and genius for your big moment?

We Love this Word

A sports term honors those who do just that. The baseball great whose batting average leaps with runners in scoring position. The few who have found the secret of being their best when it matters most are called clutch. A standard definition of clutch is: /kluCH/ to grasp (something); to seize; to take hold. One who seizes the moment of great importance. One who takes hold of the game when the opposition is formidable and the outcome matters greatly.

We move this term from the sports arena to any arena that matters to you. Here is our definition:

CLUTCH

To be your best when it matters most.
To bring your strongest effort to your biggest challenge.
To conquer your personal Everest.

In the next few chapters, we will look at the secret of the clutch performance in simple, step-by-step detail so you can implement it successfully. Later, we'll see how it can be fun,

DR. MARK POWELL

giving you the ability to recover, providing additional reserves of energy alongside a surprising sense of peace and inspiration.

But first, we need to consider something with which you are almost certainly familiar, the performance phenomenon referred to as *the zone*.

CHAPTER *two*

GET IN THE ZONE

*"But in the zone,
the extraordinary capacities that lie within
each individual are made manifest."*
- Andrew Cooper

Bill Russell called it levitating.

The basketball hall of famer was one of the first to openly acknowledge the phenomenon of the zone on the hardwood. In his autobiography *Second Wind: The Memoirs of an Opinionated Man,* Bill Russell wrote, "It was almost as if we were playing in slow motion."[2]

Warren Miller, known for making ski and snowboard movies, recently released a movie called *Flow State.* Miller set out to capture the magic of the zone on film. Lance P. Hickey, Ph.D. describes it:

> You are skiing down a mountain trail in Aspen, Colorado - one of the expert diamond slopes, with the awe-inspiring snow-capped Rockies in your view. Though you have skied down this slope before, you have never been able to "dominate" it - until now. You begin to hit your stride, striking every mogul perfectly, effortlessly. Your actions seem frozen in time and every little sound becomes more intense - the crisp slap of your skis against the powder, the scrunch of your knees, and your rhythmic breathing. You are flowing down the slope, and later you might even describe yourself as having become "one with the mountain."[3]

You too, have been in the zone. Maybe not on a mountain in Aspen. Maybe not on a basketball court. But you've been there. Perhaps you were writing a paper in college. Suddenly you were functioning with elevated brilliance and concentration. You were on. At your best. Better than your best. You were careful not to do anything that might break the spell. Perhaps it happened when giving a sales presentation or when you were participating in a test of physical endurance. You were clutch. But how do you get there? And more importantly, how do you get there whenever you want? Let's consider some insights into the zone phenomenon.

CLUTCH

The Zone and Beyond

Baseball great Ted Williams and Wimbledon champion Arthur Ashe were both clutch. Each is credited with being the first to place the zone into the lexicon of sports. The zone is the common term used to describe a heightened state of consciousness that great athletes and high achievers experience. Andrew Cooper, author of *Playing in the Zone*, writes, "All athletes know it, strive for it, prize its attainment. It is that realm of play in which everything - skill, training, mental discipline - comes together, and players feel themselves lifted to a level of peak performance in which limits seem to fall away."[4]

In 1982, James Loehr wrote about the zone. He called it "ideal performance state."[5] When athletes are asked what they feel while in this state, this is what they commonly say:

I feel relaxed.
I feel energized.
I'm fearless.
I am extraordinarily aware.
My focus is sharp.
I'm in control.
The game slows down.

Additional insight into the zone comes from the work of Hungarian psychologist Mihaly Csikszentmihalyi. He called the zone *Flow* or *State of Flow*.[6] Do forgive me for quoting Wikipedia this once. Here is how the everyman dictionary of everything described it on one particular day when I looked it up.

"...a feeling of energized focus, full involvement, and enjoyment in the process of the activity."

"...the ultimate experience in harnessing the emotions in the service of performing and learning."

"...emotions are not just contained and channeled, but positive, energized, and aligned with the task at hand."

"The hallmark of flow is a feeling of spontaneous joy..."

Two things jump out at me from Csikszentmihalyi's research. First, it's not just for athletes. At the risk of sounding impossibly broad, the zone will help anybody attempting anything.[7] Steven Kotler speaks of this and agrees, "Everything...from baking a chocolate cake to planning a vacation to solving a differential equation to writing a business plan to playing tennis to making love."[8]

Second, before Csikszentmihalyi's research, the zone was just a path to peak performance. Csikszentmihalyi introduced another benefit of the zone. Happiness.[9]

This is not an outcome-based happiness, but the joy that arrives during the challenge and effort. (Look for the term *emotional effervescence* later when we talk about fun, expanding happiness in the direction of optimism and confidence.)

CLUTCH

The zone brings peak performance for anyone and a shot of happiness. If we could tap into the zone every day, even for brief moments, what a game changer that would be.

But how do I tap into the zone and become clutch? Let's look at a useable protocol for entering the zone, documented in dozens of university studies and practiced religiously by hundreds of high achievers from Ben Franklin to Ben Affleck to Ben Bernanke – as well as people not named Ben. We are ready for the personal power ritual.

CHAPTER *three*

THE PERSONAL POWER RITUAL

"Rituals equal results."
- *Tony Robbins*

We'll call it a protocol.

In 2006, an article appeared in the Journal of Applied Social Psychology. It revealed the work of a team led by Michaéla C. Schippers and Paul A. M. Van Lange. They studied 197 top athletes, men and women, from four sports. The research showed that over 80% of these highly-accomplished athletes used one particular protocol to tap into the zone. The study found when the game had higher stakes, when their opponent was more formidable, when athletes most needed a clutch performance, they became even more committed to the protocol. The study concluded the protocol was effective and should be taught by coaches to young athletes.[10]

In 1986, researchers Lobmeyer and Wasserman studied the use of this same protocol on a random group of people who were not top athletes. One group shot free throws with it, one without it. Conclusion? The protocol improved free throw shooting accuracy.[11] A separate study by Van Raalte, Brewer, Nemeroff and Linder conducted a near identical test on putting a golf ball. The protocol proved effective once again.[12]

So top athletes and average people both perform sports tasks better with our so-called protocol. But what if you're not concerned about sports? Harvard Business School researchers Michael I. Norton and Francesca Gino tested the protocol's power to help people bounce back from failure and losses in general, things like relationship break-ups and business defeats. We'll consider this more fully in a later chapter on the power of recovery, but for now, let's note the conclusion: the protocol helps people more quickly regain control, confidence and optimism.[13]

Norton and Gino broke additional ground with a side bar discovery: the protocol works even if one doesn't believe in it.[14] It works. Just do it. The protocol puts the person using it into the zone. The zone allows you to be clutch.

The protocol in each of these studies, plus dozens of similar studies, is ritual.

Personal Power Ritual = Zone
Zone = Clutch

I know. I know. I know. You were hoping for something else.

CLUTCH

Let's face it. The word "ritual" brings to mind odd folk practicing mystical, religious and utterly strange behavior. (Can you smell burning incense?) I hope the word ritual will soon bring to mind other people. Highly accomplished people. People like Muhammad Ali, Elizabeth Gilbert or Tom Hanks. Successful people using little, positive, everyday personal power rituals to enable them to better do their thing.

Personal Power Ritual

A positive routine plus ceremony,
repeated to elevate skill, focus,
energy, confidence and happiness.

You probably have a brother-in-law who is an anthropologist. Okay, maybe not. But if you did, he could explain to you over a beer that ritual is a cornerstone of his work in anthropology.

"A ritual has two parts," he might say. "A positive routine, and ceremony."

He might ask you to tell him about the great group of close friends you are always talking about. When do you all get together? Where? How often?

He's either lonely and looking for an invite, or for part one of your friendship ritual - positive routine.

Positive Routines

Some routines are tired paths leading nowhere. Positive routines are the infrastructure of success. Positive routines need more love, and we'll give routine its due when we consider where the power of ritual comes from. Positive routines will play a part in every chapter in section two and are especially featured in The Power of Bandwidth and The Power of the Familiar. They help you have energy for the really important decisions. They cut through psychological tensions. They are that good. They are underrated as tools of achievement. You can think something through one time. Plan it out perfectly. Decide when and how you will do it. Then do this beneficial behavior without thinking about it again.

Positive Routine

A predetermined series of autopilot activities that can be repeated indefinitely to reach goals and positively shape one's life.

One last crazy good thing about positive routines versus the darling of the self-help industry, habits. Habits are jackasses. Hard to break. Hard to train. Hard to shape. Hard to create. Routines are German Shepherds. Smart, quick, eager, and so willing to work on your behalf.

So back to your brother-in-law. You describe your positive Friday night friendship routine. You arrive at your favorite pub at 6:10 each week and gather with your 5 friends.

"I'm not convinced that's a ritual," you say, poking the brother-in-law bear.

"It's not," he says. "Not yet, anyway. Now we need to talk about your ceremonies."

CLUTCH

Ceremony

These words might describe the elements of a routine. Practical. Functional. Orderly. Ceremony is completely different. Switch now to the other side of your brain.

Ceremony is one of those words many of us have trouble defining. We know it when we see it, but here are the bigger questions. Why are the most important moments of our lives the most ceremonial? What does ceremony do? Ceremony elevates consciousness.

One of the most poignant moments of the modern Olympics had nothing to do with competition. It occurred during the opening ceremonies for the 1996 Summer Olympics in Atlanta. Everyone knew he had Parkinson's disease, yet there he stood. Holding that Olympic torch, visibly shaking, Muhammad Ali worked to get the flame in the right part of the caldron so it would fire up. For what seemed like eternity he couldn't do it. Couldn't make it light. The watching world held its collective breath. Then he got it. In the words of Cal Fussman, "The flame erupted and so did hearts around the world."[15]

Ceremony elevates consciousness. What does that mean? It means that ceremony causes us to focus and feel. In the late eighties, I moved from the Midwest to the Virginia side of Washington. I was awed by the super cool things to see and do. For example, when the kids in this area go on their school field trip to the local museum, the local museum is the Smithsonian. There is the annual lighting of the White House Christmas tree on the Ellipse. (The President comes out to throw the switch.) The famous Easter Egg Roll held on Easter Monday. The Fourth of July fireworks on the National Mall. The awesome Marine Corps Silent Drill Team and troop reviews at the Iwo Jima Memorial every Tuesday night during the summer.

One day I asked my buddy Jon, who had lived in Washington all his life, to point me to the greatest of all the Washington experiences. Without hesitation or equivocation, Jon answered my question. Then he added, but you may not ever have the opportunity to attend.

It was many years later, but finally I experienced what Jon had described. A wonderful friend of the family passed. I was invited to read a passage from the Bible at the graveside. My friend was a retired three-star general. He was buried at Arlington. A full honors funeral at Arlington may be the most powerful ceremony on American soil. The Army honor guard at attention. A team of six white horses pulling a black artillery caisson upon which rests the flag-draped coffin. A riderless horse. A lone bugler, far in the distance, playing taps. Soldiers firing rifle volleys.

Ceremony

*Symbolic behavior performed to
focus and inspire.*

"So," says your brother-in-law, "do you guys have a secret handshake or something you do or words you say every Friday night? Anything that sets you apart from the other folks at the pub?"

"Well," you admit, "when we first arrive we ask who had

something great happen this week? Whoever had the best week celebrates by saying these words. 'First round's on me.'"

And you know he's got you.

We informally embrace rituals all the time, and the formal rituals are even more clear: a Presidential Inauguration, the exchange of rings at your son's wedding, the tassel toss at your daughter's graduation, the golden shovel dig at a church ground breaking. Ceremonies:

- summon our emotions
- focus our attention
- bring us into the moment
- remind us of who we are
- connect us to other people
- give us pause
- elevate our spirits
- inspire the achievement of our goals
- signify value, weight and importance

But they don't always have to be public or for a group. For the sake of your personal goals, you should become a ceremony maker. (Don't worry, you won't need to find an artillery caisson.) Studies show that even simple ceremonies are powerful from the very first time they are performed. The Harvard Business School research mentioned earlier showed, for example, this little ceremony can help a person bounce back from a loss. First, write down the loss or failure on paper. Second, sprinkle salt on the paper. Third, tear up the paper and throw it away.[16]

People who performed this ceremony got their mojo back faster than people who didn't. That ceremony could be replaced with hundreds of different little ceremonies. The active ingredient is not paper. It's not salt. It's ceremony.

The Algorithm

So it's time. (The evidence is there: you don't even need to believe it will work.) Start with a pre-determined, logical, functional, positive routine (R), setting your body in motion without draining your decision-making energy. Add ceremony (C) that is uniquely personal, symbolic, and inspirational, stirring your focus and feeling. Now repeat (n). Here is the clutch algorithm.

$$(R + C)^n = \text{Clutch}$$

You are closer than ever to being clutch.

CHAPTER *four*

WHO NEEDS TO BE CLUTCH?

"Rituals, anthropologists will tell us, are about transformation. The rituals we use for marriage, baptism or inaugurating a president are as elaborate as they are because we associate the ritual with a major life passage, the crossing of a critical threshold, or in other words, with transformation."
- *Abraham Verghese, M.D*

Twenty-three million Americans watched.

Eleven Republican candidates stood behind eleven podiums. The podiums were dramatically positioned in front of the retired Air Force One of Reagan's presidency. Imagine needing to rise to THIS occasion. (Ronald Reagan proved what a single debate performance could do. With four perfect words, as if from an Aaron Sorkin script, Reagan made history. Turning toward President Jimmy Carter, Reagan said, "There you go again."

Could these candidates live up to his legend?)

Hours before the Air Force One debate, I flipped channels for pre-debate coverage. NBC, MSNBC, CNN and FOX were paraphrasing the same question to each candidate. What rituals will you enact before the debate? The assumption was clear. With so much on the line, they'd better have one.

Personal Power Ritual Guinea Pigs

Although not an anthropologist, somehow I have spent the last 30 years researching ritual theory. My initial fascination was with the impact of positive rituals on families. My family became guinea pigs. I made little family rituals and waited to see what would happen. Eventually my friends were made unwitting guinea pigs. The impact of simple rituals upon these groups astounded me. I observed how little rituals quickly strengthened the bonds between people in small groups. Ritual experts swore this would happen. But you know how it is. You don't really get it until you experience it for yourself.

My research led me to an unexpected discovery, a discovery made 100 years earlier by French anthropologist Emile Durkheim. The rituals didn't just strengthen the group, as a group. The group rituals strengthened the individuals. You build the ritual, but then the ritual builds you. Positive rituals take on a power of their own from which the enactors draw strength. Durkheim discovered, for example, people who were members of a group with a high level of ritual were less likely to commit suicide.[17] Ritual theory explains that when a group repeats simple, positive ceremonial routines, group members develop the following:

CLUTCH

Resilience

Focus

Self-Confidence

Self-Discipline

Optimism

Happiness

This link between small group ritual and personal accomplishment may sound slightly familiar. Every couple of years, some university publishes a new study on the power of a family dinner. (They may or may not use the word *ritual* but their work is proof of ritual theory.) The results are so remarkable they get airtime in the first hour of *Today* and *Good Morning America*. A congenial host describes the surprising benefits of a four night per week family meal ritual. School grades bounce upward. Dangerous and reckless adolescent behavior trails off. Everybody gets happier and more confident and more positive. Family dinner power is preventative and corrective. So it's never too late to start.

My own findings were equally remarkable, leading me to wonder about the power of individual rituals. Could a personal ritual produce a similar elevation of emotional strength and personal performance?

I needed better mornings. Win the morning, win the day. I wanted to get in the zone for my day. I wanted to run my business in the zone to optimize my performance and happiness. I made a morning personal power ritual. It worked.

I loathed weightlifting. I loathed even more the idea of

becoming a wimp. I wondered if some sort of personal power ritual could inspire me to go to the gym and lift. Could a simple ritual make the gym a positive experience? I made the ritual. It worked. Before long Lifetime Fitness was my jam. (Feel free to replace *jam* with the latest, greatest, hippest term that I won't discover for another couple years.)

Most notably, I desperately wanted to end 16 years of fantastic failure. I wanted to run. The Boston Marathon, perhaps? No. I just wanted to get up on Thanksgiving morning and run the Virginia Run neighborhood Turkey Trot 5K. Sixteen years I tried and sixteen years I failed using popular online training programs. Year seventeen, I abandoned those training programs and made a personal power ritual for building up to running three miles. I call it Power Ritual 5K. PR5K got me into the zone and kept me in the zone for my run. I'll tell you that story a little later.

After these personal power ritual successes, one great question remained. Is it possible to make a personal power ritual for what many people say is their toughest challenge, weight loss? You may want to skip ahead to the "how to" section on weight loss. Resist. Resist. That section will be much more beneficial if you first read the preceding chapters.

Big Game Moments

Those were some of my big game challenges. Now let's focus on you. What is your thing? Your difficult challenge? Your big game? Perhaps you are...

CLUTCH

- A professional baseball player in a hitting slump
- A salesperson with a big opportunity
- A surgeon seeking greater focus and confidence in the operating room
- A college student wanting to get in the zone for exams
- A runner training for her first marathon
- A dieter needing to shed 50 pounds
- A CEO who needs to become a better public speaker
- A high school teacher seeking to be more zen

The Clutch algorithm can help. But what does the algorithm look like in your everyday life? Turn the page to find out.

EXERCISE

Your Personal Power Ritual

• • •

The purpose of this book is to help you be clutch. My goal is to help you rise to your big game challenge while enhancing your happiness. Since this book is about you, go ahead and personalize it. Write all over it. Jot ideas in the margins. Underline and highlight. Use the exercises and white space in any way that is helpful to you.

What ideas have grabbed you so far?

How could you benefit from increased focus or self-discipline?

Where could you be helped by more self-confidence or optimism?

CHAPTER *five*

START BUILDING YOUR $(R + C)^n$

• • •

My favorite sports movie is Hoosiers.

Hoosiers came to a theater near you in 1986. The hardwood hero was the fictional character Jimmy Chitwood. That year, Indiana was head over heels for their real life Jimmy Chitwood. Steve Alford. Alford averaged 37.7 points per game in his senior year and was named Mr. Basketball for the state of Indiana. In 1987, Alford led Indiana University to a national championship. His coach Bobby Knight said Alford got more out of his natural talent than any player he'd ever seen.

Alford is considered one of the greatest free throw shooters in the history of the game. His free throw ritual began with touching his socks, then his shorts, there was a pause and the ball was released.

Hoosier fans called it out.

"Socks. Shorts. 1-2-3 Swish."

• • •

Let's build your personal power ritual.

Recall our definition. A personal power ritual is *a positive routine plus ceremony, repeated to elevate skill, focus, energy, confidence and happiness.* $(R + C)^n$ = Clutch.

What is your big game? What challenge is most important to you right now? In what endeavor could you most benefit from greater *skill, focus, energy, confidence and happiness?*

Perhaps you identified a one and done challenge like taking a big test, giving an important speech, participating in your first Iron Man or interviewing for the job of your life. Or, perhaps you identified more of an everyday challenge like healthy eating and regular exercise, positive parenting, or improving your performance at work.

Don't think your challenge might be ritual resistant. It's not. Personal power rituals are equally effective for a one and done challenge, an everyday challenge or something in between.

After identifying your big game challenge, the next step is creating a repeatable positive routine.

Develop Your (R) Routine

Remember our definition. A positive routine is *a predetermined series of autopilot activities that can be repeated indefinitely to reach goals and positively shape one's life.* Start jotting down a few practical and functional elements of your new routine. Here are some of my favorite routines of the famous that helped each of them do their thing.

Each morning after coffee with her husband, the American poet **Maya Angelou** left the lovely comforts of her home to write in stark rooms at budget motels.

CLUTCH

NBA super shooter **Ray Allen**, for his entire professional basketball career, had this game day routine. First, he took a 90-minute nap at 11:30. Ate chicken and rice at 2:30. Shaved his head at 3:30. Then he headed to the court to practice.

Scary novelist **Stephen King** explains, "I have my vitamin pill and my music, sit in the same seat, and the papers are all arranged in the same places. The cumulative purpose of doing these things the same way every day seems to be a way of saying to the mind, 'you're going to be dreaming soon.'"[18]

Actress **Jennifer Aniston's** work day. She awakens at 4:30. Drinks hot water with lemon. Meditates for twenty minutes. Drinks a protein shake. Then Jennifer works with a personal trainer, spins and does a bit of yoga.

Your new routine will protect you. It will prevent you, as my mother used to say, from running around like a chicken with your head cut off. Pulitzer Prize winner Annie Dillard speaks of how a schedule or routine "defends from chaos and whim. It is a net for catching days."[19]

Have you started to scratch out a few ideas for your new routine? Some things you need to start doing? Excellent! Yeah, you! Little things make a big difference. For example, if you plan to walk or run first thing in the morning, consider setting out your running shoes the night before. You'll be surprised how that ultra simple routine inspires you. (Later I'll tell you about the popular #flatrunner Instagram power ritual.)

Now it's time to bring your routine to life. Time to make it compelling, exciting and inspirational to you. Let's add your secret ingredient.

Craft Your (C) Ceremony

Last night I watched game one of the NBA Finals. Cleveland vs. Golden State. LeBron James vs. Steph Curry. The last thing before taking the court, **LeBron James** performed his routine of chalking both hands. Many of you know what's coming. LeBron performs the famous ceremony that declares King James has come to play. He throws chalk dust into the air.

Ceremony elevates consciousness. Ceremony is *symbolic behavior performed to focus and inspire.* Ceremony turns routines into rituals.

Evocative for You or Exclusive to You

Your ceremony is totally yours. It is just for you. Craft your own. (If you try to copy LeBron you'll be cleaning up chalk dust for weeks. I was tempted too.) As you select elements of your ceremony, look for something that is either evocative for you or at least exclusive to you.

Evocative for You

Evocative elements come from your story. You lift them off the pages of your unabridged autobiography. An evocative element reminds you of something important, significant or powerful. It may be something good or not so good. Whatever it is – it somehow encourages, inspires, motivates or strengthens you.

Here is an example. Remember when men's basketball shorts were short? You know who changed the trend? **Michael Jordan**. He wore short shorts when he played in college and won the national championship at North Carolina. He wore long shorts when he played for the Chicago Bulls simply to cover up the Carolina Blue national championship shorts under his Chicago Bulls shorts. They were his Tar Heel totem. Only Michael knew exactly what this ceremonial element meant to him.

Exclusive to You

Another way to craft your ceremony is with elements that are not really evocative, but they are exclusive to you. Something original, maybe a little unusual or unique. Be creative. It could become your signature. It sets you apart. It makes you feel special – which, of course, you are.

American author **Thomas Wolfe** found a ceremonial element to inspire his work and make him feel special. Wolfe, who was six and a half feet tall, penned all his novels standing up, using a refrigerator as a desk. And, oh yes, almost forgot, he was buck naked. (If any of you were leaning in that direction - sorry, already taken.)

Here are the four most common types of ritual ceremonies used by clutch performers.

Food Ceremony

Most of you will choose something evocative or exclusive that involves food or beverage. Food ceremonies are, by far, the most common power ritual ceremonies. Yours may be what food you eat, how you eat it, where you eat it, when you eat it, or all the above.

Beethoven ground exactly 60 beans for his cup of morning coffee. NHL player **Claude Giroux** ate a grilled cheese before each hockey game because when he was a boy his mom grilled him one before each game.

Clothing Ceremony

All Superman Halloween costumes come with this warning label, *"This garment does not enable you to fly."*

Why is that warning necessary? Because what we wear influences how we think and feel about ourselves. When I was a kid, the must-have shoes made this promise.

> *Run Faster*
> *Jump Higher*
> *PF Flyers*

My PF Flyers made me run my hardest. As you build your personal power ritual, definitely consider the inspirational power of special garments.

Tiger Woods wore a red golf shirt for every final round since turning pro in 1996. **Steve Jobs** wore all black for Apple product introductions. **Serena Williams** wears the same pair of tennis socks for an entire tournament. **Reggie Jackson**, baseball's ultra-clutch Mr. October, wore just one batting helmet throughout his career. Each new team would repaint it for him.

Your clothing ceremony could involve what you wear (evocative or exclusive), how you wear it, when you wear it, the order you put it on, or even how you lay it out the night before.

CLUTCH

Music Ceremony

Music grabs emotions. Eric Clapton once said music made him ten feet tall. That feeling can help you in your personal power ritual.

The music ceremony is part of the home field advantage in Major League Baseball. Home team hitters select walk-up music, a 15 second inspirational riff played on their way to the plate. Yankee pitcher **Mariano Rivera**, maybe the greatest closer ever, entered each home game to Metallica's Enter Sandman. His ritual became one of the most powerful fan rituals in the history of Yankee baseball. Psychologist Jonathan F. Katz, quoted in the New York Times, explained "Music is a factor in getting people in the right mind-set. . . . The better the physical and mental state that the batter is in when he gets in the batter's box, the better position he is to hit."[20]

Personal Care Ceremony

One could argue the personal care ceremony, as a component of the strong performance, can be traced back to the biblical Fabio-esque superhero named Samson. Have you noticed male athletes in big games are rarely clean shaven? There must be something about growing hair that makes men feel tougher.

Women and men can either ramp up or down their usual personal care as appropriate for a big game. Just do something evocative for you or exclusive to you.

Although these four categories of performance ceremonies are quite common, there are many other options. Don't limit yourself. You will come up with something that works for you.

DR. MARK POWELL

Bring It All Together

Let me wrap up this chapter by telling you about my very first personal power ritual, created for final exams in grad school. It brought functional routine and inspirational ceremony together.

At the time, I didn't know the first thing about personal power rituals. Nonetheless, I accidentally created one (you probably have too). In my early 20s I was in graduate school where much of my grade for any class would hinge on how well I navigated the final exam. I started taking final exams seriously. I didn't know about ritual theory or getting into the zone. But somehow I knew that I needed to transform myself for those exams. I needed to step into a phone booth as Clark Kent and bound out as Superman. So I did. Kind of.

The test taking personal power ritual started in my apartment the night before the big test at around six o'clock. I studied in my little office until midnight. Then I packed up my books and papers and headed to an all night restaurant called Perkins. Upon arrival I ordered breakfast - eggs, bacon, pancakes and lots of coffee. I studied at Perkins until 4:00 a.m. and then headed home for a quick nap. When my alarm went off my only effort at personal hygiene was brushing my teeth. Didn't shower. Didn't touch my hair. Didn't wash my face. Didn't shave. I wore contacts in those days because of severe near sightedness and would not be caught dead wearing my heavy glasses. Except during final exams. I dressed in wrinkled sweats pulled from my hamper. I arrived on campus almost unrecognizable to my teachers and friends. I looked like a vagrant. Campus security

CLUTCH

may have been alerted.

Did it work? Perfectly. I had stumbled upon a personal power ritual. I still remember how I felt during those exams.

I felt confident.
I felt in control.
I felt the game slow down.

EXERCISE

Your Personal Power Ritual

• • •

Over the next few years, I imagine you crafting a dozen personal power rituals for a dozen big game challenges. Let's start with one. Below are a few possible categories to get you thinking. Perhaps one will leap off the page. Brainstorm below.

- Big Assignment

- Imposing Test

- Big Speech or Presentation

- Athletic Goal

- Kindergarten to Medical School

- Workweek Challenge

- Personal Fitness

- Making New Friends Challenge

Clutch

SECTION *two*

DR. MARK POWELL

CHAPTER *six*

INTRODUCING POWER

"The miracle isn't that I finished.
The miracle is that I had the courage to start."
- *John Bingham*

Personal Power Ritual.

We made it a *ritual*. We made it *personal*. It is time to reveal the *power*. I have had the opportunity to help many people develop and use personal power rituals. I always ask them to promise to circle back and report results. Almost everyone reports the same thing. The boost they got, the power they experienced, the benefit they received exceeded expectations. Three dozen academic studies conclude this type of ritual is powerful. Nonetheless, we are always surprised. Even me.

DR. MARK POWELL

Not Steve Prefontaine

Heads up all you natural runners and super gifted endurance athletes. Attention you out there with those long, lean, fast-twitching, octane-oozing leg muscles who look like you could line up alongside American Pharaoh and have a shot at taking him in the first 100 meters. You whose mother fondly retells that from the day you could walk, you ran. I'm not one of you. I'm not Steve Prefontaine. Never was. My mom kindly retold that when I was a boy I sat down to put my pants on. I claim that my Little League coach said, "That Mark, he may be small, but he sure is slow." I'm a natural born sitter. But I wanted to run.

I have long cared about fitness. For me personally, running was my benchmark of fitness. If I could run two or three miles before collapsing in a heap on my neighbor's fescue, I considered myself somewhat fit.

The Turkey Trot – Year One

When I was about 35 years old, our family moved into a Virginia neighborhood that proudly hosted each Thanksgiving morning a Turkey Trot 5K. Our Turkey Trot sold out annually with more than 1000 runners. We moved in during springtime in the early 90s and I declared loudly, "I'm going to run the Turkey Trot." How tough could it be? I had six months to work my way from couch sitting to running 3.1 miles. I could not have been more resolute as my training began that summer. I thought, as soon as I work up to running about two miles, I will pay my $35.00 and officially enter the race. (I figured the excitement of race day would pull me through the additional mile.) My

CLUTCH

training hit a wall at the one mile pole. I didn't sign up for the Turkey Trot that year. I watched the race from the neighborhood sidewalks. I was disappointed not to be a runner.

The Turkey Trot – Year Two

The next August I said to myself, Mark, this running thing is ridiculous. Of course you can run. Last year was a fluke. Only thirty-six years old. Generally fit. Play a little tennis. Play a little golf. Walk on an inclined treadmill. There is no reason I can't train gradually to run the 5K Turkey Trot in three months. Guess what? I failed again. In training for the Turkey Trot I never could break the one mile barrier.

The Couch to 5K Training Program

This cycle trying and failing repeated without variation for 12 consecutive years. Does the definition of *insanity* come to mind? After 12 years on the hamster wheel of fitness failure I went for help. I googled how to learn to run. I quickly discovered that I had been doing it all wrong. Apparently, I was the last person on earth to unearth the ubiquitous *Couch to 5K* in two months plan. Seems there were millions lying on couches dreaming about getting up and running 3.1 miles and someone had perfected the way to do it. I could not have been happier to find this new approach.

Couch to 5K works like this. Over the course of 10 weeks you alternate walking and running three times each week. You gradually walk less and run a little more. What a plan. I can do this! The plan instructions told me this was really easy and I'd be tempted to go farther and faster but I shouldn't. Just go slow. Stick to the plan. This will be a cinch. I followed the plan with religious determination. But at 1.5 miles I hit the wall. For the next five years, I reloaded *Couch to 5K* every summer with the Turkey Trot in my sights. I never could run more than a mile and a half without stopping. For 17 years I watched the race from the sidewalk. Churchill said, "Never, never, never give up." I was ready to hang up the shoes.

I don't blame you if you're thinking I'm making this up. Scout's honor. (I really was a Boy Scout. There was a merit badge for running. I didn't get one.) Now I'm 52. September brought my annual impulse to train for the Turkey Trot. I knew *Couch to 5K* wasn't going to work for me.

The Power of Ritual

I had an idea. How about a 5k personal power ritual? I knew about the power of rituals, but never considered creating one to help me run. I used the algorithm. Routine plus ceremony, repeated.

On September 4th, I began training using my freshly minted personal power ritual. My plan was exactly like the previous 17 years. Run three times a week. Work up to two miles. Then run the Turkey Trot on Thanksgiving. I was determined. I was not optimistic.

My first run was three blocks. By the end of October, I was running eight miles. My son and I ran the Veterans Day 10K around the Tidal Basin in Washington, D.C. Yes, I finally ran the Turkey Trot.

CLUTCH

As you might imagine, I was stunned by my accomplishment. Stunned by the power to run in the zone provided by my personal power ritual. I never would have succeeded at running without it. Later, in the fitness section, I will explain all the details of my ritual. But don't skip ahead. I believe it is important to attempt to understand why rituals work. How is it that these simple rituals are so powerful? Years of ritual research have led me to five distinct power benefits of a ritual. Five power benefits that help you enter the zone. Five power benefits that help you become clutch.

The next five chapters explain the five power benefits. As you read these five chapters, don't feel like you need to modify your personal power ritual to make it powerful. Since you followed the algorithm, these five power benefits are ready to be discovered.

CHAPTER *seven*

THE POWER OF FUN

"People rarely succeed unless
they have fun in what they are doing."
- *Dale Carnegie*

My first keynote speech on *Clutch* was followed by audience Q&A. I was jazzed when lots of hands shot up. People were excited about what they learned. But quickly the whole thing went south. It was my fault. I screwed up. A few of the questions revealed a problem with my talk. A big problem. Somehow I had allowed the audience to think a personal power ritual was some kind of rigorous practice of self-discipline. (Did my inspirational clothing list reference sackcloth?)

Here is what I forgot to say to that crowd. *This is going to be fun.* It's going to be fun because a PPR increases effervescence, enjoyment and happiness.

Effervescence: Bedtime

One of the first to discover this was the French anthropologist Emile Durkheim. I like the word he used. Durkheim said rituals produce *effervescence*. (Think enthusiasm, excitement and liveliness.) More recent research by Michael I. Norton and Francesca Gino produced this assessment by Norton. "We see in every culture – and throughout history – that people who perform rituals report feeling better."[21]

But don't take their word for it. Conduct your own research. It's easy. If you are a parent or grandparent of a young child, use our algorithm $(R + C)^n$ to make a bedtime ritual. Start with things like brushing teeth, changing into PJs and putting clothes in a hamper. Then be sure to add ceremonial things like saying special words, singing a little song, or doing a little dance. Do this three nights in a row. Look at the face of that little boy or girl. What do you see? That's effervescence.

Enjoyment: Carrots and Wine

A study reported in the September 2013 issue of *Psychological Science* examines how small ceremonies or rituals performed before eating changed the perceived taste of food.[21] In one study, two groups of people were given instructions on how to eat carrots. Group One banged their knuckles on the table, closed their eyes, and took a deep breath before eating each carrot. That's "routine plus a ceremony, repeated." A ritual. Group Two did three random actions before the first carrot, three different random acts before the second carrot, and a whole new set of random acts before carrot number three. That's not a ritual. So which group reported the greater enjoyment of their carrots? You guessed it. The ritual made the carrot taste better and made the experience of eating it more positive.

Further studies were conducted with lemonade and chocolate. (Thankfully, not together.) Every study showed that performing a ritual enhanced the experience of eating.

Maybe the idea of a fancy-tasting carrot sounds silly, but let's think about fine wine and the added enjoyment that comes with a sommelier. Once the host places his or her order, the sommelier presents the bottle and repeats the name and vintage. The foil is cut at the second or lower lip and tucked into the sommelier's pocket. The top of the cork is wiped with a clean serviette and removed quietly. A one-ounce taste is poured and handed to the host for approval.

Sure, the waiter could slop wine into glasses and bring it out. But there's something about that ritual that produces anticipation, and ultimately, enjoyment.

Then the glasses are raised. Cheers!

Happiness: A Key to Success

Rituals produce happiness. We are not talking about the happiness that comes from entering the zone. That brings an additional happiness. We are not talking about the happiness that comes from better outcomes. That is another happiness. Just performing your personal ritual gives a micro-dose of happiness.

All things being equal, a happy person is more successful. Full stop. Shawn Achor documents this finding in his book *The Happiness Advantage*.

For untold generations, we have been led to believe that happiness orbited around success. That if we worked hard enough, we will be successful, and only if we are successful will we become happy. Success was thought to be the fixed point of the work universe, with happiness revolving around it. Now, thanks to breakthroughs in the burgeoning field of positive psychology, we are learning that the opposite is true. When we are happy – when our mindset and mood are positive – we are smarter, more motivated, and thus more successful. Happiness is the center, and success revolves around it.[23]

The bottom line? Happiness leads to success.

As you begin road-testing your personal power ritual, consider keeping a little mood diary. You might be surprised to find that you are more joyful and enthusiastic, but I wouldn't be surprised at all. Studies reveal that rituals produce enthusiasm, positivity, mood elevation, joy, hope and self confidence. That's effervescence, enjoyment and happiness working for you. Fun.

On to the power of recovery.

CHAPTER *eight*

THE POWER OF RECOVERY

"Success is how high you bounce
when you hit bottom."
- *George S. Patton*

High expectations accompanied swimmer Matt Biondi to Seoul for the 1988 Summer Olympics. He was to be the new Mark Spitz. Swim seven. Win seven. Gold medals, that is. But it was not to be. A devastating third place bronze in his first event was followed by a disappointing silver medal in his second.

Sportscasters agreed that this might crush Biondi. He might not win a single gold. Biondi was still talented enough, but they thought those early losses would derail him.

One man knew better: Martin Seligman, the famed psychologist working with the American swim team. On a few occasions, Seligman explicitly informed swimmers their time was slower than it actually was. Every swimmer on the American team followed up their "fake slow swim" with a "real slow swim." Every swimmer except Biondi. Failure made him faster.

After bronze and silver, Biondi won five gold.

Years later, Biondi was asked how he pulled victory from the proverbial jaws. He said, "I had a clear choice to make: to swing to the positive or the negative."[24] I would like to know if Biondi had any sort of comeback ritual, or if he made the swing just by deciding to make the swing. For most of us, quick recovery from failures and setbacks will require more than a decision to be positive. It will require action.

Rituals and Recovery

Your thing is probably not the breaststroke. Whatever it is, I want you to be well prepared for failure and setback along the way. Failure is part of the game.

Actors act badly.
Writers get blocked.
Quarterbacks throw interceptions.
Hitters strike out.
Politicians step in it.
Sales people lose big deals.
Students get disappointing grades.
Geniuses do dumb things.
Ace pitchers give up home runs.
Dieters eat donuts.

CLUTCH

The clutch fail too. They just recover quickly. A personal power ritual is a recovery tool. This research can again be tracked to Durkheim who found rituals made people emotionally resilient. Family dinner research shows the same.

The most useful research on this topic is an academic journal article entitled *Rituals Alleviate Grieving for Loved Ones, Lovers, and Lotteries* by Michael I. Norton and Francesca Gino.[25] Here is their conclusion. Loss makes us feel out of control. Rituals act as a psychological mechanism, helping us regain the feeling of control and renewed optimism. The following are three of their discoveries that will help you understand and implement your personal ritual.

Any Recovery Ritual Helps

Norton and Gino write, "Rituals of mourning in the face of loss – from the death of loved ones to the end of meaningful relationships to losses in wars and competitions – are ubiquitous across time and cultures."[26] Every culture has recovery rituals but they're not all the same. One culture does a certain thing to recover. Another culture does the exact opposite. The recovery power, therefore, is not in any specific ritual element. It is in performing a ritual.

Recovery Rituals Need Action to be Effective

Norton and Gino instructed people who had experienced a small loss to sit in silence and reflect. They explained that this is one way people have traditionally responded to loss, but this did not help the test subjects recover.[27] The psychological mechanism that powers recovery involves taking action. One must *do* something to regain the feelings of control and renewed optimism.

Recovery Rituals are Homemade

The study revealed that people who experienced personal losses benefited from inventing personal, private recovery rituals. Only rarely did people adopt the rituals of others. Like with apple pie, recovery rituals are better homemade.

Your Personal Power Ritual Has Recovery Power

Norton and Gino studied special rituals made specifically for loss recovery, but Durkheim's research found that all meaningful rituals help people recover. This means your personal power ritual has built-in recovery power. But you may need more. Depending on the nature of your big game, you may also need a quick, in-the-moment recovery ritual. Imagine a soccer defender or keeper who gets in the zone by using her pre-game personal power ritual. Halfway through the game she struggles after allowing a goal. She needs to bounce back right then. A predetermined, quick, special recovery ritual would help.

I'll never forget watching an interview with Evander Holyfield shortly before his championship fight with Mike Tyson. A sportscaster asked Holyfield how he saw the fight going. His analysis proved prophetic. Holyfield said, if he hits me clean, I'll go down. If I manage to hit him clean, he'll go down. If I go down, I'll get up and fight on. If he goes down, it's over. He has never come off the canvas to win.

Sooner or later we all get hit, but here's the good news. Your new personal power ritual contains a psychological mechanism that enables you to come off the canvas and win. You have the power of recovery.

Next, the power of the brain and the will. We'll call it bandwidth.

CHAPTER *nine*

THE POWER OF BANDWIDTH

"Fifty percent of baseball is half mental."
- Yogi Berra

• • •

President Obama has two suits.
The two are exactly the same except one is solid navy and the other is solid charcoal. Michael Lewis wrote a piece for Vanity Fair about President Obama's every day life. President Obama explained to Lewis that the job of the president is to make hard decisions. The easy decisions never reach the Oval Office. Obama continued, "You'll see I wear only gray or blue suits. I'm trying to pare down decisions. I don't want to make decisions about what I'm eating or wearing. Because I have too many other decisions to make."[28]

• • •

When you started building your personal power ritual (routine plus ceremony, repeated), the very first piece you put in place was your routine. As I mentioned earlier, routines don't get the love they deserve. You've heard people say something was *just* routine. For some people, routine means ho-hum. Those folks may be surprised to hear that science has proven a routine can increase one's bandwidth. That means your PPR gives you more brainpower and willpower. Sound too good to be true? Hang with me and I'll show you what I'm talking about.

Your PPR Will Increase Available Brainpower

William James is considered the father of American psychology. In his work, *Psychology: A Briefer Course,* James says the more we hand over the small details of daily life to the effortless custody of automated routines, the more higher brainpower will be available for our important work.[29] The simple act of making decisions degrades our ability to make further decisions.

You might assume that James' interest in this topic meant that he was himself a master of the well-ordered, routinized life. Exactly the opposite. He was talking about himself when he wrote:

> There is no more miserable human being than one in whom nothing is habitual but indecision, and for whom the lighting of every cigar, the drinking of every cup, the time of rising and going to bed every day, and the beginning of every bit of work, are subjects of express volitional deliberation. Full half the time of such a man goes to the deciding, or regretting, of matters which ought to be so

CLUTCH

ingrained in him as practically not to exist for his consciousness at all.[30]

My Misery

When I set out to write this book, I struggled. I felt like I did when I once attempted to sail off in a boat that was cleated to the dock. Every Monday morning, I tried to block time for writing. It went like this.

> *Okay, I'll write on Friday. Twelve hours straight. That's what I'll do! But wait. Would it be better to write first thing every morning? But I'm more relaxed in the evening. Excellent. The evening it is! Some authors binge write. They go off for two or three weeks and knock out the whole thing in mountain cabin solitude. I'll Google, "Mountain Cabin Rentals by Owner for Struggling Authors." (MCRBOSA.com) I hear Stephen King writes 2000 words a day, every day, even on his birthday. Stephen King wrote Misery. I wonder what it's about. Maybe it's about an author who can't start writing.*

All my brainpower was exhausted by the when-and-where-to-write decision. Thus, I did not have the bandwidth to write. I proved this William James quote true, "Only when habits of order are formed can we advance to really interesting fields of action."[31] I eventually framed the "routine" part of my PPR. Soon words appeared on the page.

DR. MARK POWELL

Your PPR Will Increase Available Willpower

Raise your hand if your greatest strength is your willpower. (I'm not sure any hands went up, but in the event yours did, you can put it down and use it to turn to the next chapter.) Roy F. Baumeister, a social psychologist at Florida State University, cites a million-person survey on personal strengths and weaknesses.[32] What do you suppose was the number one personal weakness? Lack of willpower.

Has anything like this ever happened to you? It's January 2nd, Day One of your New Year, I-Really-Mean-It-This-Time Diet. You do pretty well at breakfast. You stay on course through lunch. It's now six o'clock. You're driving home from work. You're getting hungry. No food at home. No plan for dinner. You stop at Trader Joe's. Your hungry brain evaluates a thousand items in the store. Do I like that? What does that taste like? Is that healthy? Is it true that I should eat chocolate every day? How many calories in that bag? Isn't apple pie mostly fruit? Is that a self-limiting food or one where the more I eat the more I want? Is that going to take an hour to prepare or can I eat half of it before I reach the checkout stand? All your willpower bandwidth is depleted in the shopping process.

In her book *The Willpower Instinct,* Kelly McGonigal reveals that what is true of brainpower also applies to willpower. There are limits. McGonigal writes,

> Now more than ever, people realize that willpower—the ability to control their attention, emotions and desires—influences their physical

health, financial security, relationships, and professional success. We all know this. We know we're supposed to be in control of every aspect of our lives, from what we eat to what we do, say and buy. And yet, most people feel like willpower failures—in control one moment but overwhelmed and out of control the next. According to the American Psychological Association, Americans name lack of willpower as the number-one reason they struggle to meet their goals.[33]

Every morning, you have lots of fresh available willpower bandwidth. Throughout the day, every act of self-control, self-restraint, or self-discipline depletes your willpower bandwidth until none remains.

McGonigal writes, "Welcome to one of the most robust, if troubling, findings from the science of self-control: People who use their willpower seem to run out of it. Smokers who go without a cigarette for twenty-four hours are more likely to binge on ice cream. Drinkers who resist their favorite cocktail become physically weaker on a test of endurance. Perhaps most disturbingly, people who are on a diet are more likely to cheat on their spouse."[34]

But not everything good and productive whittles away at willpower bandwidth. For example, you wake up and immediately brush your teeth. Check your bandwidth. Still plenty available. Highly automated routines use little or none.

An automated routine is like an external force. It's like the moment you step on a moving walkway at the airport. You've been rushing through the airport, steering your wheeled bag, and then you hit the walkway. It sweeps you along and you feel exhilarated, fast. Your effort decreases, yet your speed increases. Durkheim called this power sui generis, meaning it was a power outside of you, not sucking your bandwidth.

In his book *Daily Rituals: How Artists Work*, Mason Currey said it this way, "A solid routine fosters a well-worn groove for one's mental energies and helps stave off the tyranny of moods."[35]

Take a moment and think about the big game you identified. Would more brainpower – higher brain functioning – help you succeed? Certainly! Would extra willpower advance your cause? You bet it would! Your personal power ritual gives you both - more bandwidth.

Next up, the power of the familiar.

CHAPTER *ten*

THE POWER OF THE FAMILIAR

"To engage in a ritual is to settle in to a familiar algorithm of life in which each step follows the preceding step with gratifying predictability."
- *J. N. Nielsen*

You are what you repeat.

Aristotle brought that to our attention. Repetition shapes us in obvious ways. If you start lifting weights for two hours each day, a year from now you will be shaped differently because of that repeated effort. But there is another, maybe less apparent, benefit of repetition. Repetition creates familiarity. Familiarity will help you eliminate high stakes errors. Let me show you how.

Schippers and Van Lange point out that clutch performances are routinely undercut by one thing: psychological tension.[36]

When the game really matters, even top performers report restlessness and self-doubt. They are insecure. How do you solve that? Dr. Jens Kleinert, sports psychology professor at the German Sports University Cologne explains that repetition makes the athlete feel secure.[37] Doing something familiar and comfortable before or during a big game, test or performance has been proven to relieve the psychological tension.

Dr. Bradley J. Cardinal, a professor and co-director of the Sport and Exercise Psychology program at Oregon State University says it's about bringing the familiar into the unfamiliar. "World-class athletes prepare for different scenarios and the routine helps them keep the situation normal, no matter what is happening around them."[38]

One of the best descriptions of the power of repeating a ritual comes from blogger J. N. Nielsen,

> To engage in a ritual is to settle in to a familiar algorithm of life in which each step follows the preceding step with gratifying predictability… there is no more settled form of thought than that prescribed by a ritual. Not only can our actions follow a familiar course of predictable steps, but our thoughts too can be ritualized, falling into a comfortable rhythm of a familiar sequence of ideas in which the equilibrium of one's mind is not disturbed. Ritualistic thought is perhaps a kind of meditation. Rituals, then, may comfort us because they are familiar and they help to keep us

CLUTCH

calm and peaceful in the midst of a chaotic and unpredictable world.[39]

The familiar repeated action on the occasion of the biggest of big games can give you a moment when you say to yourself, *I've done this 100 times. Today really is no different. I've got this.*

I think that is what **Coach John Wooden** had in mind. He began the first practice of the UCLA basketball season by asking his players to be seated. He then showed them the proper way to put on their socks and shoes. Coach Wooden knew, if all went well, the season would end in March Madness. Those players would arrive in a strange place to play for a national championship. In an unfamiliar locker room, they would experience psychological tension and waves of adrenalin like never before. In that moment, every player knew exactly what to do. They sat down and put on their socks and shoes the UCLA way. UCLA, under John Wooden, won an unprecedented seven consecutive national championships.

Serena Williams plays tennis around the world. The cities change. The crowds change. The courts change. Here's what doesn't change.

1. Her socks. Just one pair per tournament.
2. She laces her shoes unconventionally.
3. Bounces the ball exactly five times.

She uses the power of the familiar. She is ready to play.

CHAPTER *eleven*

THE POWER OF INSPIRATION

"Sometimes a symbol holds more power
than the thing it represents."
- Jarod Kintz

I call it Truffaut's Ceremony.

François Truffaut, legendary French film director, began his career by walking three blocks from his apartment to a small bookstore. There he purchased a book on how to direct a film. I don't know the title. Perhaps *Film Directing for Dummies.* Truffaut returned home with the instructional book, read it and set out to direct his first film. With more success, more opportunities came, but this walk and book purchase became his ceremony. Before each subsequent film shoot began, Truffaut would leave his apartment, walk three blocks to that small bookstore, repurchase the same book on how to be a film director, and would again read the book. Only Truffaut knew exactly what this ceremony meant to him, but we can guess it gave him either a sense of focus or inspiration, providing what is needed to begin, and begin again.

We appreciate the power of grand social ceremonies. They demand our attention, reminding us of our calling, healing our wounds, and boosting our resolve. But many of us don't take advantage of the power of small personal ceremonies in our daily lives. The power of the most majestic ceremony resides in your new personal power ritual. Let's recall our definition, a **ceremony** is *symbolic behavior performed to focus and inspire.* Ceremony is ceremony whether it is elaborate or simple, corporate or personal.

Get Ready to Run

I like everything about a ritual ceremony that has caught fire in recent years. The night before a race, runners lay out, with crime scene precision, their running clothes: perfectly laced shoes, socks tucked into shoes, shorts, shirt, bib, four safety pins, hats, gels, and so on. The #flatrunner is photographed and posted on social media. Runners say this is inspiring, helping them get up for the challenge.

Your ceremony may be much more simple. Simple is just fine. Here is your take-away. The power of inspiration contained in the most elaborate ceremony is available to you. So use it. It will help you enter the zone. It will help you be clutch.

Wrapping Up the Five Sources of Power

Like I said at the beginning of chapter 6, I have had the privilege of helping hundreds of people, including good friends and family members, build personal power rituals for varied purposes. I ask them to circle back and tell me how it's going, and they do. They say things like, "You won't believe how well this worked." The power of a personal ritual takes everyone by surprise. Even *I'M* surprised every time I create a new one. So even though I have told you what to expect; even though we've considered how powerful a personal ritual can be, how it can be fun and help you recover, giving you bandwidth, a sense of the familiar, and inspiration, you won't really get it until you try it. Look forward to being delighted.

EXERCISE

Your Personal Power Ritual

• • •

Before moving on, take a moment to reflect on how you could benefit from the five powers.

The Power of Fun. Think of an important endeavor, task or challenge that you do not enjoy. Perhaps one you procrastinate. Do you think it would be possible to make it more enjoyable?

The Power of Recovery. In what area of your life do you experience failure, setbacks and disappointment? Where could you most benefit from a quick recovery?

The Power of Bandwidth. If you had to choose between more daily brainpower or willpower, which one would you pick?

The Power of the Familiar. When do you feel anxious and uncomfortable? When might you benefit from gratifying predictability?

The Power of Inspiration. Truffaut needed inspiration at the start of new directing projects. When do you need inspiration?

Clutch

SECTION *three*

DR. MARK POWELL

CHAPTER *twelve*

PERSONAL POWER RITUALS IN ACTION

"Of all the virtues we can learn
no trait is more useful, more essential for survival, and more
likely to improve the quality of life than the ability to transform
adversity into an enjoyable challenge."
-*Mihaly Csikszentmihalyi,*
Flow: The Psychology of Happiness

I love YouTube.

YouTube has become the go-to resource for the do-it-yourselfer. Instead of reading about how to smoke a turkey in my Big Green Egg, I can watch a few videos of Egg Heads *showing* me how they do it.

We are all Missourians. We like *show* more than *tell*. We say to our friends, "Show me how you do it." This chapter is about showing you how people like you have used the principles of *Clutch*.

DR. MARK POWELL

Story of a NICU Nurse
Story of a Keynote Speaker
Story of Becky and Match.com

By the way, I know many have identified getting fit as your big game. That's fantastic. This chapter does not include a story of creating a fitness or weight loss ritual only because the final section of *Clutch* is completely dedicated to that important challenge.

The Story of a NICU Nurse

Abby's big game is her job. She works twelve hour shifts as a neonatal intensive care nurse at a major metropolitan hospital. Not only could most people not handle doing what she does, most people could not handle hearing about it. Dangerously premature babies. Parents in crisis. After a decade caring for her precious patients, Abby began to feel compassion fatigue. As is not uncommon in nursing, she was feeling burned out.

After hearing about personal power rituals, Abby created the following ritual to reinvigorate her nursing practice.

Part one. Abby bought new special socks for work. She chose Balega running socks because a friend told her they are the world's finest running socks. Abby feels that by wearing high quality socks she is taking care of herself so that she can take care of her patients.

Part two. She switched radio stations for the drive to the hospital. Rather than listening to news or the local shock jock, she listens to a Christian radio station. The inspirational music

CLUTCH

and encouraging commentary put her in a positive, peaceful frame of mind.

Part three. Right before work, Abby sends out a good morning text to her daughters. This could be her last chance to reach out for a while. By signing off communication to her kids, Abby feels free to focus all of her attention on her patients.

Part four. Scrub in with Francis. NICU nurses are required to do a 2 minute hand scrub before their shift. Abby memorized the prayer of Francis of Assisi to recite silently during scrub in.

> Lord, make me an instrument of thy peace.
> Where there is hatred, let me sow love;
> Where there is injury, pardon;
> Where there is doubt, faith;
> Where there is despair, hope;
> Where there is darkness, light;
> Where there is sadness, joy.
>
> O divine Master, grant that I may not so much seek
> To be consoled as to console,
> To be understood as to understand,
> To be loved as to love;
> For it is in giving that we receive;
> It is in pardoning that we are pardoned;
> It is in dying to self that we are born to eternal life.

When I interviewed Abby, I asked what her ritual does for her. "I feel my anxiety flows out of me and I have a very strong sense of peace in this chaotic environment. I feel purpose. The ritual clears out the noise and allows me to focus on the needs of my patients and their families."

The Story of a Keynote Speaker

Charlie makes millions as an author and keynote speaker. Each year he flies around the world to address some of the world's largest companies and conventions. Last year, his fee for a keynote ranged from $14,000 to $32,000. If all goes well when he speaks, he can make another $10,000 to $15,000 in book and product sales. Charlie's keynote speeches are his big game.

Charlie, like every public speaker, actor, comedian, litigator, or school teacher can tell you about the magic of the zone. The experience is not work. It is play. He is painting with words. Creating art in real time. Connecting almost individually with each person in the audience. Time changes. Time always slows to your advantage in the zone. Charlie explained to me that he created a personal power ritual to increase his "in zone speaking percentage." He estimated that before his personal power ritual he was in the zone for about 35% of his speeches. Really off for about 10%. Somewhere in between for the other 55%.

Charlie's ritual had three easy parts.

Part one. Charlie did a full rehearsal the morning of each talk. The entire talk, start to finish, was presented as well as possible to the furniture of his hotel room. He did this for the same reason Jerry Seinfeld rehearsed his first Tonight Show stand up routine 200 times.

Part two. Charlie had a favorite solid gray suit. He decided to wear that suit for each keynote and never to wear it for any other occasion. He had a favorite pair of black shoes that he shined before each talk.

Part three. Charlie did not want to come off as a showboat, superstar speaker. He wanted to connect. He wanted to be authentic, vulnerable and real. The final part of his ritual was to arrive early for his speeches and mingle with his audience. (Before this, he had remained isolated in the green room and reviewed his notes before he spoke.) He would try to learn the names and stories of five people. If possible, he attempted to give his talk to those five – making direct eye contact with his five new friends repeatedly.

In addition to feeling in the zone about 50% more, Charlie reported that somehow speaking became more fun.

The Story of Becky and Match.com

When you think about big game moments, you may not have included that moment where you meet someone at a bar or party or in the produce aisle at Whole Foods. A moment when even the silky smooth can become the ever awkward. For my friend Becky (name changed so my friend doesn't shoot me), that was exactly the big game moment for which she sought help. Becky found herself single again after 14 years of marriage. Her last first date was 17 years ago. A friend on the next street over kept telling Becky to try the popular dating site Match.com. "No way!" was her response. Like many people, Becky was hoping a friend would match her up or she would bump into Mr. Wonderful at church or in the elevator at work. It wasn't happening.

She decided to give Match.com a shot. One brave night, Becky typed in her credit card digits, created a pleasant, girl-next-door profile, uploaded seven *fairly* recent photos and pressed *Post*. Within an hour she felt like a high school cheerleader. Every few minutes a new email arrived saying, "Hello...let's meet for coffee or maybe a glass of wine."

The idea of meeting strange men for the purpose of finding a match was both exciting and terrifying. She was hoping she would be her best, most engaging self while being acutely discerning of the character and intentions of the men she met. At my suggestion Becky created a power ritual for these dates.

Part one. Becky whitened her teeth with Crest Whitestrips while she was getting ready. Whitening her teeth helped her feel like she was pampering herself and putting her best foot forward.

Part two. Becky wore a horseshoe necklace that her mother had given her. The necklace was more than a good luck charm to Becky. It represented her greatest passion growing up, horseback riding. She was fully alive and fearless when harnessing 1000 pounds of horse power. The necklace reminded her of her strength and confidence.

Part three. Becky texted her best friend, "Nobody puts Baby in the corner (or the trunk!)" before she left for her dates. The quote is a play on a line from Dirty Dancing, Patrick Swayze's line to Jennifer Grey's character, Baby, when he pulls her up on stage to dance with him. It was both a comedic reference to a favorite movie and a practical way to communicate that she was headed out so that someone close to her knew that she was on a date.

CLUTCH

Part four. Becky stopped by the Bojangles drive through on her way to meet her dates and ordered and ate a biscuit. Munching on a flaky, buttery Bojangles biscuit in the Bojangles parking lot was a yummy way for Becky to avoid drinking on an empty stomach and helped ensure that she wouldn't be tempted to extend a first date beyond a single drink because she was hungry.

Flash forward 22 months. Wayne proposed to Becky on bended knee on the rail at the Kentucky Derby as the thoroughbreds thundered by. The two were married nine months later. (Yes, biscuits were served at the reception!)

CHAPTER *thirteen*

**WIN THE MORNING
WIN THE DAY**

"Each day is a little life:
every waking and rising a little birth."
- *Arthur Schopenhauer*

Schopenhauer's words resonate with me.

Every waking *is* a little birth. Every new day *is* a little life. Waking up triggers the start of something new and fresh. Because of this, no matter what your thing, your Everest, or your big game, I want you to think about how crafting a morning power ritual might lead to better mornings and better days.

Many have observed the key to unlocking the rich potential of each new day is the morning. The first moments. Win the morning – win the day. I love mornings. I have spent twenty-five years reading every book promising even a nugget of insight on how to win my mornings and I found almost universal agreement among the experts. The key is your morning ritual.

Tim Ferriss, the author of the best seller *The Four Hour Workweek*, hosts a podcast where he interviews high achievers for the purpose of deconstructing their secrets of success.[40] Ferriss always asks, "What is your morning ritual?" Ferriss seems to assume that accomplished people are likely to have robust morning rituals.

Peak performance guru Tony Robbins agrees. Robbins recommends a 60 minute morning ritual. He calls it your *Hour of Power*. Robbins says if you can't do the *Hour of Power* morning ritual, go with *Thirty Minutes to Thrive* or *Fifteen Minutes to Fulfillment*.[41] I want to encourage you to give it a shot.

Mornings Differ Radically

Let me acknowledge a glaring reality. Our mornings differ. The word morning means something different to each of us. First, we can't agree on when a proper morning starts. Some people claim to "get up early." They roll out of bed at 7:30. Others claim to "sleep in late." They bound to their feet daily at 6:00 sharp.

Second, some of us have days that ramp up around 9:00 or 10:00. Others have two-hour commutes beginning at zero-dark-thirty. I know new parents who are up repeatedly through the night. I know single moms who hold down demanding jobs with early starts while also having three small children to get dressed, fed, hugged and onto a yellow bus. That single mom may be the one who most needs a better morning. She most needs a morning power ritual – even if the ritual is performed in her car at red lights or on a Metro bus.

A Morning Ritual is a Gift

A morning ritual is one of the greatest gifts you can give yourself. It is time for you. You have heard the silly line, *We're not human doings. We're human beings.* Your morning ritual is a gift of time to be. Great morning rituals are as different as the people who enact them. But great morning rituals all have one attribute. They are positive. They are something you look forward to. A great morning ritual will help you wake up like it's Christmas. In one talk about morning rituals Tony Robbins said, "It doesn't feel like discipline, it feels like joy."[42] My children tell that when they were growing up, our family had wonderful morning rituals each Saturday and Sunday. The kids say that when they misbehaved, they were punished by being allowed to sleep in.

> "It doesn't feel like discipline,
> it feels like joy."
> -Tony Robbins

Alexandre Dumas, the writer of *The Count of Monte Cristo* and *The Three Musketeers* found joy and inspiration each morning by eating an apple under the Arc de Triomphe.[43] Writer **Gertrude Stein** found her morning inspiration by just going out and sitting in her car.[44] Whatever you choose, make it a joyful experience that makes you want to rise and shine.

A Morning Ritual Gives Time to Think

I listened as a speaker referenced a survey of 100 people who had celebrated their 100th birthday. They were asked, knowing what you know now, what would you have done differently throughout your life? One of the top answers was, "I would have reflected more."

Another survey of 100 CEOs asked, what do you wish you had more time to do? The answer was, "Think." They longed for time to think about the big picture issues of life and business.

When **Margaret Thatcher** was the British prime minister she carved out a time to reflect and think each morning while listening to a BBC radio program called *Farming Today*. It was a program about, well – farming.

Summer mornings. Winter mornings. Autumn mornings. Spring mornings. Every morning is a wonderful time to reflect. Your morning ritual gives you time to think. (I think best with a black, medium point, Paper Mate Flair and yellow legal pad.)

A Morning Ritual Gives Time for Gratitude

Jump start your day with gratitude. **Tony Robbins** spends three minutes each morning focusing on three things for which he is grateful. He attempts to feel gratitude with his whole being for three minutes. He says, "…gratitude is the antidote to the things that mess us up. You can't be angry and grateful simultaneously. You can't be fearful and grateful simultaneously. So, gratitude is the solution to both anger and fear…"[45]

Nothing rewires your brain quicker or better than gratitude. See what happens if, for one week, you list things for which you are thankful within 30 minutes of waking. Your little gratitude ritual. Zig Zigler said, "Gratitude is the healthiest of all human emotions. The more you express gratitude for what you have, the more likely you will have even more to express gratitude for."[46]

UCLA neuroscience researcher Alex Korb has studied how gratitude changes our brains. The antidepressant Wellbutrin bumps up the neurotransmitter dopamine. Prozac bumps up the neurotransmitter serotonin. Gratitude is a shot of dopamine with a serotonin chaser. Gratitude bumps up both. Korb explains that you don't even have to be grateful to get the bump, just seeking to be grateful is highly effective and every attempt to be grateful will make you more grateful in the future.

> It's not finding gratitude that matters most; it's remembering to look in the first place. Remembering to be grateful is a form of emotional intelligence. One study found that it actually affected neuron density in both the ventromedial and lateral prefrontal cortex. These density changes suggest that as emotional intelligence increases, the neurons in these areas become more efficient. With higher emotional intelligence, it simply takes less effort to be grateful.[47]

Practice gratitude and gratitude will grow.

DR. MARK POWELL

Your 100 Minutes of Genius

You are allotted 1,440 minutes each day. Have you noticed those minutes are not created equal? Many have discovered a time of peak creativity, insight and wisdom. I call it *100 Minutes of Genius*. In these moments, we are Bradley Cooper in *Limitless*. (He swallowed a magic pill giving him cosmic creativity.) You may discover your 100 minutes happen in the morning, after a good night's sleep.

My 100 minutes are from about 8:00 to 10:00. Once I discovered my 100 minutes, I determined to use them well. I don't need genius to pay bills or do the laundry. Tim Ferriss of *Four Hour Workweek* fame speaks about the *Maker Brain vs. Manager Brain*. Your normal brain can *manage* all day long. So use your 100 minutes of genius to *make*.

Benjamin Franklin had a two-hour morning ritual. Part of his ritual was always list-making. One list item daily was his *powerful goodness*. He asked, "What good shall I do today?" Imagine if you devoted your minutes of genius to responding to that question.

Win Your Morning

You alone know what it means to win your morning. Only you know what sort of positive productivity, cosmic creativity or powerful goodness is your ideal. Whatever you attempt each morning, pursuing it with the help of the personal power ritual algorithm should make a noticeable difference.

EXERCISE

Your Morning Personal Power Ritual

• • •

Your big game personal power ritual, the one you have been working on, may happen first thing every morning. If so, use this space to consider tweaking that ritual. But it's possible that your big game personal power ritual is not a morning thing. In that case, you might want to think about creating a separate personal morning ritual as gift to yourself. Either way, use that pen in your hand to reflect.

- When might your morning ritual happen?

- How might you practice brain-changing gratitude every morning?

- What would be your best and highest use of your 100 minutes of genius?

Clutch

SECTION *four*

DR. MARK POWELL

CHAPTER *fourteen*

CLUTCH FITNESS INTRODUCTION

"I spent my childhood eating.
The only exercise I got was trying to twist off the
cap from a jar of mayonnaise."
- *Richard Simmons*

Did you identify fitness as your big game?

Have you struggled for years with losing weight, eating healthy and exercising regularly? *Clutch* is not the be-all, end-all resource on diet and exercise. If you don't really know what healthy nutrition looks like, you may want to work with a nutritionist. If you don't really know what a balanced exercise program looks like, a personal trainer might be a good investment. Most likely, you learned long ago that leafy green vegetables are better for you than Cheetos. You probably have a pretty good idea what a balanced program of cardio, stretching and lifting looks like. The problem isn't knowing what to eat. The problem isn't knowing how to exercise. The problem is doing it.

Clutch can help.

This fitness section of *Clutch* will deal separately with two major components of fitness. We will start with the easy part. Exercise. How to find motivation to move and make it fun. Then, we will provide you with a shiny set of new tools to work on the stubborn challenge of diet.

Clutch and Exercise

One friend of mine updates me weekly on his training progress for the Hawaii Ironman. Other friends speak of wanting to simply introduce a little walking into their weekly schedules. No matter what your exercise plan happens to be, a personal power ritual (routine plus ceremony, repeated) will advance your cause.

No doubt you have occasionally had to push yourself to get up and exercise. You know the feeling. The internal struggle. You think of 100 reasons not to exercise. At least not now. You exhaust yourself with a closely-scored mental debate. Exercise wins by a nose. You push yourself hard and off you go.

Your personal power ritual for exercise should transform that "self-push" into a *sui generis* pull. You will start to feel drawn to your exercise routine by an outside force. Like suddenly your best friend in the whole world – whom you haven't seen for years, who is fun and funny, positive and encouraging – suddenly shows up at your house and says, "Let's go hiking together like we used to. Get your clothes changed. You and me. One great hour. Let's go!" Your friend gets you moving, keeps you moving, and makes the whole experience more fun.

Clutch and Food

Before sitting down to write this morning, I went on a 4 mile hike. I walked beside the Potomac River. When I got back home, I literally checked the "exercise" box on my legal pad. That box will remain checked. No one can un-check that box.

Eating is a different challenge. How many times have we eaten perfectly from the time we awaken until say, 10:15 at night? Right before bed, in just five minutes, we go from a 500 calorie daily deficit to a 500 calorie daily surplus? In five minutes of late night snacking, we uncheck the "eat healthy" box. (By the way, a 500 calorie daily deficit leads to losing 52 pounds in a year. A 500 calorie daily surplus leads to gaining 52 pounds a year.) Eating right is our 24 hour challenge.

Clutch can help you with this challenge in a unique way. Here is the big idea. All eating is ritual. We wrongly speak of our "eating habits." They are not actually habits. They are powerful rituals. Our eating - the way we eat, where we eat, what we eat - is routine plus ceremony, repeated. Many of the ceremonies began in childhood. Food is symbolic.

Therefore, the best way to change a powerful eating ritual is to replace it with another powerful eating ritual. That's what this section of *Clutch* will help you do.

CHAPTER *fifteen*

MY RUNNING BREAKTHROUGH

> "Somebody may beat me,
> but they are going to have to bleed to do it."
> *- Steve Prefontaine*

Have you always wanted to enjoy a nice morning run? Have you flipped through articles on your phone explaining how one hour of running adds seven hours to your life? Have you heard that no other activity increases lifespan like running? And yet, you don't run. I know how you feel. That was me. I wanted to run.

> **"Check with me
> before starting any new exercise plan."**
> *- Your Doctor*

DR. MARK POWELL

Each year, for 17 years in a row, I set out each fall to get off the couch and work up gradually to running 3 miles. Each year I failed, always hitting a wall around the one mile mark. Then I created a personal power ritual to help me run. With power from my ritual, in just two weeks, I ran two miles without stopping. I was astounded. Eight weeks in, I ran eight miles without stopping.

A personal power ritual is routine plus ceremony, repeated. Here are the details of my running ritual.

Time to Run

The first element was *time*. I ran at 8:30 in the morning, always on an empty stomach. Time was such an important part of the ritual that it took me years before I got to the point where I could run any time of day.

Dress for Success

The second element was *clothing*. I bought new Nike running shorts and top rated Balega Hidden Comfort running socks. I had good shoes from my failed attempts. I wore the exact stuff for each run. No decisions to be made.

Power Running Home

The third element was *place*. Where I ran was a game changer for me. Have you ever ridden a horse? Horses want to run as they approach their barns. It occurred to me that I might get an emotional lift by running toward my house. My mailbox became the finish line. My street is three blocks long. On day one, I could only run about three blocks. I walked three blocks down my street, turned around and ran the three blocks back to my house. Made it without stopping. Good beginning.

On day two, I walked those same three blocks and then added three blocks more. I ran the six blocks back to my house. It may seem that running six flat blocks is running six flat blocks. It doesn't really matter where those six blocks are located. But it does matter. I intentionally chose to run from unfamiliar to familiar. This was a powerful reversal from what I had done for 17 years. The section of the run where I would be most tempted to quit, the section where my new personal record was to be set, always occurred on the familiar and comfortable home stretch. The three blocks of my own street. The three blocks that I had run successfully from my very first day. The three blocks during which I had never given up.

Day three. Same pattern. Walk out nine blocks and then run home. I continued the walk out and run back approach until I was up to 1.5 miles. From then on I no longer walked before the run. I started my run at my mailbox and ended at my mailbox. I still added three blocks on each run. I continued to set my personal long run record on those same familiar three blocks of my street.

The Power Song

The fourth element was the *soundtrack*. The playlist. Like mainlining adrenaline. On that very first day, with only three blocks to run, I still needed a song. One might select music for its pace-setting tempo or because it makes her happy or because it takes his mind off running. I needed music with attitude. A fighting song. An against-all-odds song. A song of defiance. After 17 years of failure, I needed to run with a little piss and vinegar to succeed.

If I had known that I would one day write about this, I would have chosen my song more carefully. As in something more masculine. Perhaps the theme from *Rocky* or One Day More from *Les Mis* or something off Toby Keith's *Shock'n Y'all* or *Unleashed* albums. But here's the truth. My power song was Not Ready to Make Nice by the Dixie Chicks. I had no interest whatsoever in the politics of the song. I just connected with the attitude, especially this one lick about three-quarters through:

> I made my bed, and I sleep like a baby
> With no regrets, and I don't mind saying
> It's a sad, sad story
> When a mother will teach her daughter
> That she ought to hate a perfect stranger
> And how in the world
> Can the words that I said
> Send somebody so over the edge
> That they would write me a letter
> Saying that I'd better
> Shut up and sing
> Or my life will be over.[48]

That song made it impossible for me to quit. Not Ready to Make Nice is three minutes, 58 seconds long. When I started my running program it was my one-song playlist. As I added distance, I added songs to the beginning of my playlist. Every single record-breaking run would be timed so that as I came down the final stretch, the three familiar blocks of my street, Not Ready to Make Nice would play in my ears. I engineered inspiration. The hardest part of the run was the most powerful part of the ritual. No matter what. Regardless of how tired, how hot, how winded, how thirsty. I would never stop running until I touched the mailbox. And I never did. The power of this ritual made what had been impossible for 17 years easy and fun. I set a new personal best every other day for eight weeks.

My Original Playlist

1. Viva la Vida – Coldplay
2. Born This Way – Lady Gaga
3. Before He Cheats – Carrie Underwood
4. Live Like You Were Dying – Tim McGraw
5. How Do You Like Me Now – Toby Keith
6. Independence Day – Martina McBride
7. All Things Are Possible – Darlene Zschech
8. Not Ready to Make Nice – The Dixie Chicks

I still run. I no longer need the familiarity of that home stretch. These days I run the hills and trails of the Manassas Civil War Battlefield. I can now run without music when necessary – such as in a triathlon when music is not allowed. But still when I go for a new personal running record, I cue up support from Natalie Maines and the Chicks to get me through.

CHAPTER *sixteen*

YOUR POWER RITUAL FOR RUNNING 5K

"Run when you can, walk if you have to,
crawl if you must; just never give up."
— Dean Karnazes

I'm excited for you.

If becoming a runner for the first time or getting back into running after a long absence is your goal, then you are in for a treat. This chapter will provide the framework for a ritual that is likely to make running a fun part of your life.

The *Couch to 5K* running plan, developed in 1996 by Josh Clark, has helped many thousands become runners. This excellent plan didn't work for me for a simple reason. *Couch to 5K* focuses on the physical challenge of getting your legs and lungs into running shape. My legs and lungs were not my problem. It was my brain. My will and motivation kept giving out at the one mile pole. My legs said, "Let's go faster." My lungs said, "Let's go farther." My brain said, "Quit. Give up. Go home."

That is where a personal power ritual can help. Your personal power ritual for running should help you with the mental and motivational challenges to running. Below are suggested elements of a strong running ritual. It is not necessary that you embrace all of these elements. I still run. But since running is now easier for me, I no longer need all of these elements. I think you may find the more of these elements you incorporate into your ritual, the more powerful your ritual will be.

POWER RITUAL 5K

Run at a Specific Time

Make an effort to start your run, or any exercise, at a precise time. Remember baseball great **Wade Boggs** ran wind sprints at 17 minutes past the hour.[49] It will be more unique, powerful and engaging if you can start your runs with precision. If you can't - you can't. You want to remove as much decision-making as possible. Don't get caught in the misery of small decisions over when to run. "Should I run now? Perhaps the weather will be nicer in five minutes? I might feel more like running if I wait 25 minutes." Precision promotes automation.

Organize Your Clothes, Shoes and Socks

Even now, I have a drawer in my night stand for all my running stuff. Shorts. Shirts. Shoes. Socks. This drawer is a key to my success. You will want to eliminate the small struggle of searching for your running stuff in hampers, closets, multiple drawers or under the bed. Small struggles can be a reason not to run.

Try to wear things you really like or things that are special to you or inspire you. I ran in a Superman t-shirt for a while. Think about Michael Jordan and his Tar Heel shorts.

Have your stuff all ready the day before the run. No game time decision. If you want even more motivation, you can do what many of your fellow runners do - build a #flatrunner. Lay out your clothes and shoes the night before. Make it look as if you were lying on the floor in all your running clothes and suddenly you vaporized and your clothes flattened in place. Take a #flatrunner picture if you want.

Figure Out What to Eat Before the Run

Stan Musial was one of the greatest hitters in baseball history. Lifetime .331 average. Sixteen consecutive seasons batting over .300. On game day, Stan the Man ate just one egg, followed by three pancakes, followed by just one egg.[50]

As we have said before, food is both routine and ceremony, functional as well as symbolic. Don't minimize its power to help you achieve your running goal.

When you start your running, don't be surprised if you look for any excuse to declare, "I must stop. I can't run my distance today." It's too hot. It's too cold. It's too windy. My belly is so empty. My belly is too full. Eating exactly the same food should eliminate one of your excuses.

Increase Your Distances

If possible, run three days each week. Day One: Go for a

nice 30 minute walk. At the end of your walk, run one block or a tenth of a mile. Day Two: Run two blocks at the end of your walk. You simply add one tenth of a mile 30 times. Your 10th run is one mile. Your 20th run is two miles. Your 30th run is three miles. With each run you can shorten the walking part as you like. Every run is a new personal record. It may only be an extra tenth of a mile but it is still a new best for you.

Own Your Home Stretch

Remember that a horse wants to run to his barn. When the barn is in sight, a tired horse discovers new energy. You will too. Use this to your advantage.

For example, let's say that on running day five, you walked five blocks out from your house, turned around, and then ran those five blocks back home. A couple days later, when you are attempting to run six blocks, you walk six blocks from your house, you turn around, and run those six blocks back. (Of course you may walk farther if you like, but the run will start six blocks away from your house.)

Each new increased distance, each new personal record, happens in that same one block home stretch. The place where you are most tired and inclined to quit will be the place of greatest motivation and determination, your home stretch. You are running to the barn. You own that home stretch. You won't stop. If you can time it so the same inspirational song is playing in your earbuds for the home stretch, all the better.

CLUTCH

THREE FINAL TIPS

Never Think about Running While Running

The greatest and easiest runs are always the ones where you get lost in positive and creative thoughts. If you are thinking about running you will start thinking about quitting. Plan what you are going to think about on your run.

The First Mile is NOT the Easiest

The rookie running mistake is thinking that you feel your best at the start of your run and then worse and worse as you go along. Not usually true. Often you have to run a bit to get loosened up and feeling good. So if you start running and it feels difficult, encourage yourself. The first mile is not the easy one.

Speak Well of Running

For the 17 years I struggled to run and failed, my thought was, "I don't like running. But I need to run for my health." I was turning running into work. Running is play. You loved running around as a child. Love it again. People who run, love to run. They worry about the day when they will no longer be able to run. Running is a privilege. If you desire to run, speak well of it.

EXERCISE

Your Personal Power Ritual

• • •

Whether you are an Olympic marathoner or someone wanting to work up to a mile or two, your personal power ritual will speed you to the finish line. Jot down your initial answers to these questions.

- Ideally, when would you like to run?

- Identify one item of special running clothing that you own or need to buy.

- What one song moves you like no other?

- Write down your signature something, a unique or unusual thing you might do.

CHAPTER *seventeen*

THE CADENCE OF REGULAR EXERCISE

"To enjoy the glow of good health, you must exercise."
-Gene Tunney

• • •

I have never been more riveted to my television. One summer, on the evening of June 23, I could barely breathe as I watched him. Nik Wallenda walked a 1500 foot steel cable suspended 1500 feet above the Grand Canyon floor. Unnetted. Untethered. Only Wallenda, a cable and a pole. The engineers had pulled all the slack out of the cable. The cable was essentially a rounded beam of steel crossing the canyon.

Wallenda climbed up. Took his first step. Then another. Then another. Each foot fall the same. Same weight. Same distance. Same pressure. Same pace. Same rhythm. Soon the cadence of Wallenda's steps was picked up by the cable. The cable came to life like the string of a Stradivarius. You could see the cable taking on more and more energy. Wallenda moved the cable. Then the cable moved him.

• • •

Perhaps you've been saying, "I need more exercise," but running isn't your thing. That's okay. Neither is high wire walking. I'm with you on that one. There is some exercise that appeals to you. You want to become a hiker or biker, swimmer or gym-er, CrossFit-er or tennis ball hitter, or something else. If that is you, I'm pretty sure you are not thinking about exercise as a one-and-done. Exercise for the next six months – then remain stationary for the following six years. No. You understand the importance of exercise for life. You want to become one of those people for whom exercise is part of the cadence of life. You seek a version of what Wallenda experienced over the canyon. You want to get to the place where you can't *not* move. Where you are being moved to move. Where it is more natural to exercise than to not exercise. Where exercise becomes play, joy and refreshment. Many people do experience this. You can too. Let's work on how to get you started.

Personal Power Ritual for a Life of Exercise

We start, as always, with the personal power ritual algorithm.

$$(R + C)^n = Clutch$$

It's **(R)** routine, plus **(C)** ceremony, **(n)** repeated. Let's think through what would make a strong routine for you.

Your Exercise Routine

Routines are not all equal. The better your routine, the better your result. Here are my suggestions.

CLUTCH

Simple Wins

You may be tempted to over-engineer your exercise plan. You tend to think big. So you may be tempted to design the ultimate cross-training workout routine. Something created on a spreadsheet tracking Monday wind sprints, Tuesday Brazilian Jiu Jitsu, Wednesday rock climbing and so on. Who knows, that may be in your future. But please, start simple. Pick one thing. Power-walking. Tennis. Push-ups. Why is starting simple better? Because what you want from your routine is automation. It's nearly impossible to automate complexity. One thing, done at one time, in one way - that can easily become automatic for you. Pick one thing. Do one thing.

Exercise By Appointment

Exercise deserves a calendar slot like an important appointment. Respect it. Don't be late by even five minutes. Start precisely on time. Make your start time like an imbedded cue from a skilled hypnotist. Clock strikes your time cue. You start your appointed routine. No brainpower needed. Even better, no willpower needed.

Eliminate Uncertainty

Perhaps you've heard, "He is not always right, but he's never uncertain." That might not always be fantastic in life, but it is terrific when starting an exercise program. Be certain, be confident about the value of the exercise you have chosen.

Uncertainty cost me eight years of wasted gym membership. For those eight years I went to Lifetime Fitness – in fits and starts

- with no real plan for what I was doing there. I figured I'd just watch what other people did and do that. Terrible idea. There were 100 people doing 100 different things. Every gym visit brought the *misery of small decisions*. No wonder I avoided going.

Enter Alwyn Cosgrove. One day in 2010, I happened upon a *Men's Health* podcast while driving to a friend's wedding. The podcast guest was fitness guru Alwyn Cosgrove. Cosgrove convincingly explained that people waste lots of time at the gym. He explained that there were just seven lifts that I needed to do. These seven covered my major muscle groups. Cosgrove said, forget what other people are doing at your gym, these seven lifts are all you need. To this day, those seven are my lifting routine. I have never doubted that Cosgrove knew what he was talking about. The misery of small decisions was gone. Before long, I looked forward to going to the gym.

Succeed Early

Consider setting a goal so small that it will be impossible to fail. We are talking about creating a lifetime exercise cadence. You will have the rest of your life to add distance, time, weight or whatever. Let's get you started with an early success.

Your Exercise Ceremony

It's time for a **(C)** ceremony. Ceremony, *symbolic behavior performed to focus and inspire,* can take many forms. Like we have mentioned before, you can eat special food before or after exercise, wear special clothes for exercise, or listen to special music during exercise. Let me throw out three other simple ceremony possibilities.

CLUTCH

Smack Something

If you are exercising with friends, by all means, smack them, bump them or high five them in celebration. Dacher Keltner, professor of social psychology at the University of California, Berkeley has studied team touching. High fives, fist bumps, helmet smacks and hugs have been shown to promote winning on sports teams.[51] If you are exercising alone, smack a tree, rock, mailbox, fence, gate or dog. Remember the Harvard study that showed physical action was a necessary part of any loss recovery ritual?[52] In the same way, the physical action of ceremonial touch will make your ceremony effective in summoning your emotions, focusing your attention, and bringing you into the moment. Or if you've got dance skills, feel free to bust a great dance move to start or finish your exercise.

See Something

Another ceremonial element might be to always look at something motivational before your exercise. Perhaps a photograph of your favorite fit athlete or movie star or perhaps a picture of yourself a few years back. Or you could make a chart showing your exercise schedule or fitness goals. Both of these are ceremonial reminders of your big picture goals.

Speak Something

I grew up in Indianapolis and regularly attended what we Hoosiers simply call The 500. One of the great pre-race moments was the speaking of these ceremonial words, "Gentlemen, start your engines." I bet you could quickly come up with ten other examples of famous ceremonial words. The right ceremonial words will indeed elevate your spirit as you start your exercise routine.

I'm sure all sorts of inspired ideas and powerful possibilities are now in your head. Write them down. Refine your ritual. Plan your start. Wes Adamson, author of *Imagination by Moonlight*, writes, "Rituals are like electrically powered transmitters sending stimulating sparks of electric current or inspirational feelings that connect us to our inner being or soul."[53] Your new ritual will produce stimulating sparks. You will succeed.

EXERCISE

Your Personal Power Ritual

• • •

Below is space for your simple thinking. Start simply. Simply start. One thing. One time. One way. Before long you can be enjoying the cadence of automated exercise. Remember to seek the advice of your physician.

Describe your one thing exercise idea. If you are still winnowing down your options, write down your best ideas.

You may or may not need to eliminate uncertainty. If you do, how will you go about researching your exercise idea to be certain you are starting a good thing and doing it correctly?

You will want the "stimulating sparks of electric current" that come from adding ceremony to your exercise. What jumped out at you? Say something? Smack something? See something? Another something?

CHAPTER *eighteen*

THE MYTH OF EATING HABITS

"I was eating in a Chinese restaurant downtown.
There was a dish called Mother and Child Reunion.
It's chicken and eggs.
And I said, I gotta use that one."
-*Paul Simon*

Raise your hand if you just skipped ahead and landed here. I certainly understand. The challenge of eating and weight loss is so great that many of us can't wait to get help. Well, whether you word-for-worded your way to this chapter or took the shortcut, welcome!

Our Old Stubborn Eating Behavior

You've said these words 100 times. "I need to change my eating habits." You may have put together a change program.

First, you identified your old, unsustainable eating habits. Second, you designed your new healthy, fantastic, live-to-100 eating habits. Third, you switched out the old eating habits for the new eating habits. How did that work out? Probably, not so well. The switch didn't stick. You found yourself pulled back into the old eating habits.

Why does this happen? What's the problem? The fundamental problem is we don't understand the old eating behavior we are trying to change. We have seriously mislabeled our old eating behavior when we called it "eating habits." (For those who read word-for-word to this chapter, you are now way ahead of me. Yeah you! for figuring this out.) Your old eating behavior includes a highly-automated routine. It's Pavlovian. Ring the bell. You salivate. But your old eating behavior also includes some of your deepest and most profoundly meaningful ceremonies and symbols. You have special food for celebration. You have special food for comfort. You have food (sight, taste and smell) that evokes your favorite memories of childhood.

Your old eating behavior is a routine plus a ceremony, repeated. The old eating behavior you are trying to change is an unintended, yet still powerful personal ritual. (Remember that food eaten as a ritual tastes better.) You want to change your old eating behavior because it is not producing the health and fitness you desire. But your old eating behavior is hard to change because it is providing you with the five powers (explained in section two) of any personal ritual.

CLUTCH

The Power of Fun

Your old eating ritual is fun. Maybe wearing jeans with an elastic waist isn't fun, but the eating part is fun. Your old eating behavior has the power of fun. It produces emotional effervescence. I have come to understand that emotional effervescence is not uniquely present in sugar and fat. It is uniquely present in ritual. In order for your new healthy eating plan to work, it needs to be just as fun. Dale Carnegie said it well, "People rarely succeed unless they have fun in what they are doing."[54]

The Power of Recovery

Your old personal power eating ritual also provided you power to recover from setbacks, losses, failure or just long, hard work days. Remember the scene from the Harvard recovery study where people took the action of sprinkling salt on paper then threw the paper away? We do the same sort of thing, but we eat the salt along with the recovery burger and fries. Good news! Food doesn't need to be unhealthy to pack recovery power.

The Power of Bandwidth

Some days we arrive home hungry with no meal plan. We have pushed hard all day and we are up to here (imagine the bold hand gesture I just made) with decision-making. We experience William James' misery and so we default to automated, mindless eating. See food. Eat food.

When this happens to me I stand-up snack. I stand in front of an open refrigerator or open pantry and grab stuff. "These crackers don't crunch. How long have they been open? They're really stale. Maybe they're fine."

Mindless eating is unavoidable, but that's actually a good thing. Mindless eating is highly-automated, kicking in when your brainpower and willpower bandwidth are spent, causing you to eat what's on hand. Pick new foods to keep on hand (routine), come up with a fun way to eat it (ceremony), and let these become the highly-automated, mindless eating choices of your future.

The Power of Inspiration

Food rituals inspire. The most common ritual element used by top athletes for big game inspiration is special food. Food is emotionally evocative.

I'm working on this section while on vacation. For nearly 20 years, my family has vacationed in the tiny town of Stone Harbor on the Jersey Shore. Stone Harbor vacationers have an evening food ritual. Every summer evening, between 9:00 and 11:00, everybody goes to Springer's for an ice cream cone. The line for Springer's is the longest ice cream line you can imagine. People jam the sidewalk for two blocks along Third Street. Is Springer's the only ice cream shop in town? No. Is Springer's ice cream far and away better or cheaper than the five other ice cream shops with zero wait times? No. So why does everybody - I do mean everybody - stand in that loooong line? It's the power of the Springer's ritual. Springer's, the cone and the line, is a ceremony of summer. Springer's inspires hope. How might a new food ritual inspire you?

CLUTCH

The Power of the Familiar

Your old eating ritual is powerful just because it's old and familiar. Psychological research calls this the *mere exposure effect*. Continued exposure to a certain food makes it familiar. Familiar food produces a positive response. Familiar food comforts.

Use routine and ceremony to make the healthy familiar.

Two Big Conclusions

Let me state two encouraging conclusions that you may have already figured out. First, it is not true that junk food tastes good and healthy food tastes bad. Even though it seems you were genetically predisposed to love Froot Loops and hate fruit, it's not true. Our rituals (each routine plus ceremony, repeated) are responsible for how we feel about food. Many people in the world hate the food I most crave, peanut butter. How can this be? Ritual. Obviously, this conclusion is fantastic news.

Second, you should be feeling new hope as you transform your eating ritual to match your vision of a healthy you. You now understand that your old eating behavior is not a habit. Not a program. Not a simple routine. It's an unintended, powerful personal ritual. Only one thing can overcome it, a new, intentional, powerful personal ritual. So, let's build one for you.

CHAPTER *ninteen*

DECONSTRUCTING YOUR OLD
WAY OF EATING

"Hold it, Newman.
You wouldn't eat broccoli if it was
deep fried in chocolate sauce."

- *Jerry Seinfeld*

Israeli psychologists Daniel Kahneman and Amos Tversky won the Nobel Prize for their groundbreaking work on faulty human decision making.[22] Even if you don't recognize their names, you may have heard of some of their big discoveries: hindsight bias, anchoring and behavioral finance. They researched how our brains get tricked into repeatedly making bad decisions. In no area is this more true than with eating.

Before we start constructing new, healthy eating power rituals, let's first deconstruct your old ones. Let's see if your brain has been making good decisions for you.

Deconstruct Your Eating Behavior

You have been eating your entire life. Surely you understand everything there is to know about your old eating behavior. That's what I thought too. Turns out, I didn't. One summer I started tracking my eating experiences. I attempted to eat and think at the same time. Some call this eating mindfully. I wrote down my experiences and observations. When I ate. When I overate. I took note of my enjoyment of food. I looked for patterns and trends. I made surprising discoveries about me that helped me form my new eating rituals. I encourage you to deconstruct your existing eating behavior. Imagine you are Benedict Cumberbatch in his brilliant role as Sherlock Holmes. Observe every detail. Take special note of three things.

1. Observe Your Gastro Moods

A friend of mine likes to say, "I eat my stress." Other people report eating sadness and loneliness. I discovered that I eat my celebration. I did pretty well with my eating except on *special days* that called for gastronomical celebration. I observed that I celebrated special days like Christmas. Thanksgiving. Birthdays. Bank holidays. Chinese holidays. Jewish holidays. Christian holidays. Groundhog Day. Fridays, because the workweek was ending. Saturdays, because the weekend had arrived. Sundays, because it was Sunday. Washington Nationals wins. You get the idea. Too many special days of celebration.

Figure out what mood you eat. This will be important later.

CLUTCH

2. Observe Your Enjoyment of Foods

Daniel Kahneman and Amos Tversky introduced the world to the decision making tendency they called *anchoring*.[56] Here's how anchoring works. An instructor asks a room full of people to write down the last two digits of their phone number. Somebody may write down "00." Someone may write down "99." Most are in between. Then the group is asked to guess something. For example, the number of jelly beans in a jar. Kahneman and Tversky found that people with low phone number digits guessed low. People with high phone number digits guessed high. They irrationally "anchored" their guesses to their phone number. The instructor then showed the group what they had done. Then they were asked to guess some other number. Guess how that went. Correct. They did it again.

Our brain loves to play tricks on us with food that lead to poor decisions. So I want you to Sherlock your enjoyment of food. Observe whether you are experiencing a type of anchoring. Sometimes our brains anchor to certain foods – often high-sugar, high-fat, high-carb foods. We convince ourselves that these must-have foods give us the most enjoyment. Maybe they do. Maybe they don't. You are likely to have surprise discoveries that will shape your future eating rituals. That's what happened to me.

Before I Sherlocked my spaghetti, I was positive that my dang Hoosier taste buds blocked my path to better nutritional choices. I liked things like macaroni and cheese, fried chicken, burgers, pie and ice cream. My Hoosier taste buds didn't resonate to cod, cucumbers and cantaloupe. Given my taste bud pre-adolescent programming, I believed that in order to achieve my personal fitness goals, I would need to make a painful happiness swap. I would need to derive less happiness from eating in exchange for deriving more happiness from feeling fit.

My self-study of mindful eating produced this big surprise. The happiness, pleasure and enjoyment that I experienced from food was far less about the food than I thought. It was about whether I was hungry or not. My Hoosier mom was right. "Mark, if you are hungry, anything will taste good." The reverse is true. If you are not hungry, your favorite food brings little or no enjoyment. This simple discovery changed my game plan.

3. Observe Your Food Celebrations, Symbols and Ceremonies

Do you like birthday cake? Given what you've been reading, you are not surprised that much of the enjoyment of birthday cake is the birthday cake ceremony. Any cake recipe is significantly enhanced by candle fire and familiar song.

Last month I went on my annual sailing trip on the Chesapeake Bay with friends. I was in charge of morning coffee on the boat. I brought my coffee maker from home. I bought Komodo Dragon Blend from Starbucks. Requested the perfect grind for my paper cone filter. Executed, with pharmacological precision, the ideal proportions of two tablespoons of grounds to six ounces of bottled spring water. (Beethoven, obsessed with his coffee, hand counted exactly 60 beans.[57]) Every morning on the boat I announced, "This is the world's best cup of coffee." When my trip ended, I continued making my morning coffee exactly as I did on the boat. How many times have I announced at my house, "This is the world's best cup of coffee?" None. It was not the brew. It was the boat.

Our enjoyment of special occasions can easily be transferred to the food we eat on those occasions. Look at your favorite food through the lens of ritual. Did your mom fix you a certain food when you were a kid growing up? Do you associate a food with friends, holidays, parties or vacations? What are the stories from your life told by some of your favorite foods?

Last night I was walking in an outdoor shopping plaza with my wife. I said, "Honey, did you just smell that cigarette?" She had. I said, "I've never had a cigarette. And I don't know what brand of cigarette that was. But I know where I smelled it for the first time. It was 1968 at the Indianapolis 500 with my dad. Somebody sitting near us was smoking that exact brand."

If the smell of second-hand smoke triggers memories from the Nixon administration, how much more emotionally evocative is food you have enjoyed repeatedly? Knowing this will be helpful as we build your new eating rituals.

EXERCISE

Your Personal Power Ritual

• • •

The purpose of this exercise is the help you eat mindfully. I encourage you to observe yourself eating in the way the popular meditation app Headspace encourages people to observe themselves breathing.

- How might you go about eating mindfully and taking note for a while?

- How are your emotions and your refrigerator linked?

- Can you name a couple of healthy foods that taste great to you?

CHAPTER *twenty*

STRUGGLE AND SUCCESS

"We must have a pie.
Stress cannot exist in the presence of a pie."
-David Mamet

Transforming a lifetime of eating behavior is the ultimate challenge for the personal power ritual. By comparison, test-taking or speech-making or day-starting are easy. Healthy eating is a tough nut. It's all day, every day, for life.

When I set out to apply the principles of *Clutch* to healthy eating, I had my share of misfires. Thomas Edison encouraged me. Before eventually inventing the light bulb, Edison claimed he first invented 10,000 ways *not* to make a light bulb. I had Edisonian certainty that I was one switch flip away from seeing the light.

Like Edison, my failures educated me.

Chipotle, Chipotle and More Chipotle

Chipotle was a super success. Then it wasn't.

I sought to automate a healthy and unique eating routine. Same food. Same time. Same place. Maybe something with an unusual twist so it could become my signature ceremony. Got it. I will eat at Chipotle six nights each week. That's what I did. Soon I knew the calories of every fresh ingredient used to make Chipotle burritos. If I had a dollar for every time I said, "Yes mam, I know that the guacamole costs extra." My custom burrito bowl had 690 calories. Super nutrition. Super tasty. Super satiety. My ritual was fun. Chipotle became a happy place. The misery of indecision was gone. Cravings and hunger were gone. Before long, 11 pounds were gone.

What do you think went wrong? You guessed it. I started hating the food. I tried everything, but I couldn't eat another 690 calorie burrito bowl.

Be prepared for a bit of trial and error on this journey of self discovery. If you keep grinding, you will soon craft a healthy eating ritual that works.

Your Coming Success

The *Clutch* approach to changing eating behavior for life worked for me. I eventually got it right. You will too. Here are a couple data points intended to encourage you.

I was finally able to build an enjoyable, sustainable eating routine and ceremony with foods that I could eat and repeat mindlessly. I lost about 3 pounds a month until my BMI numbers were in the correct zone. But then, I suddenly started

CLUTCH

experiencing chronic fatigue for the first time in my life. After a month, I saw my family doctor. He couldn't find anything wrong. After another month of lethargy, I saw a specialist. She found nothing wrong. After 90 days, I saw my second specialist. He ran every blood test known. When they were all good, he asked, "Have you been eating better lately and maybe losing weight?" He figured out that as a result of my healthy eating and weight loss, I no longer should be on a beta blocker that lowers blood pressure. My blood pressure, especially when taken at home, was too low. That was it.

That was three years ago. My blood pressure is still ideal. My most recent blood work showed my bad cholesterol (LDL) at 57. That may be good enough for the Guinness Book of World Records. I should check into that.

I am happy with how this has worked for me. Now let's make it work for you.

CHAPTER *twenty-one*

BUILD YOUR WEIGHT LOSS ROUTINE

"It's never too late to become what you might have been."
- *George Eliot*

Check your mindset.

Your new eating routine needs the right mindset. A positive mindset. A growth mindset. People often launch themselves into weight loss programs with a turbo boost of shame. Can we all agree not to do that? Instead, give yourself grace. You are kind to others, be kind to yourself. No need to beat yourself up about where you've been, like you can punish yourself into health. Build this new eating routine on a foundation of self-love and self-respect. This is a wonderful new eating ritual (routine plus ceremony, repeated) that will make you healthier while also being fun, adding bandwidth and inspiration, aiding recovery and providing the comfort of the familiar. Let's do this.

DR. MARK POWELL

A Routine for Life

Here's a thought that may be new to you: the imagined future draws us to it. Martin Seligman remarked that our species has been misnamed "homo sapiens" or wise ones. Instead, we should be called "homo prospectus" because we thrive on imagining our future prospects.[58]

This could be wonderful if the future you are imagining is one of svelte-ness and healthy eating, but it will be a problem for people on a temporary diet. Here's what I mean: let's say you begin a 16 week diet. Each day you fixate on two future prospects. First, svelte-ness. You imagine reaching that new ideal weight. Fitting into those jeans. Wearing that Speedo again. (Okay, maybe not that.) Feeling more confident. Second, you imagine eating more "normal." You imagine eating some bread or a little ice cream again. Your homo prospectus brain skates to where the puck is going. Your brain pulls you into your future. Your very convincing and forward thinking brain shouts "Carpe Diem dieter! The future is now, baby! Let's do this!" Now you're eating cream puffs by the handful and falling short of that svelte new you.

Whether the diet is South Beach or Atkins or Paleo doesn't matter. Limited periods of self-deprivation rarely lead to permanent results. Here's the big picture. If a man weighs 220 it's because he eats exactly like a 220 pound man eats. If he wishes to weigh 190, he can't temporarily deprive himself and then return to 220-pound eating. He needs to start eating like a 190 pound man, and keep at it. Before long, he is that 190 pound man. The same applies to women. The *Clutch* approach is to help you make this lifelong change and enjoy it.

Laird Hamilton, legendary surfer and one of the fittest 50-somethings in the world, often says that diets never work. He emphasizes developing a plan you can live with for life.[59] Amen to that. The *Clutch* approach to weight loss is about replacing old, up-to-now eating rituals with new, from-now-on eating rituals.

A Routine of Precision

Here is a frustrating truth. If you cut out 100 calories a day, you lose 10 pounds this year. Twenty pounds in two years. That's fantastic. One hundred calories is nothing. You can easily find a 100 calorie thing to do without. The problem is that it's also easy for another 100 calorie thing to creep in without even noticing it.

Perhaps no area of your life requires such pharmacologic precision. You must know precisely the number of calories you burn each day. (I wear a Fitbit to help.) You must know precisely how many calories you eat each day. Off by 100. Gain 10.

Does this sound overwhelming, impossible, and ridiculous? Here is the secret. Eat and repeat.

A Routine of Groundhog Day

Remember the movie *Groundhog Day* with Bill Murray? (If you are the one person on earth who hasn't seen it, put down this book, pop some corn and watch it on Netflix.) Most top athletes, as well as people who look good in Spandex, eat like it is Groundhog Day. They eat the same foods over and over.

Lather. Rinse. Repeat. As Malcolm Gladwell explains in *Outliers*, repetition is essential to doing anything well.[60] Many have found the following pattern to be both doable and enjoyable. Six days each week they eat basically the same things. One day each week they eat whatever sounds good. No foods barred.

Why is this repetition necessary? Is variety bad? Not at all. But game time decisions are bad. We don't have enough brainpower and willpower, at day's end, to orchestrate, over the roars of an empty stomach, healthy, enjoyable, satisfying meals containing a very precise number of calories. Nobody can do that. So here is our goal. To the greatest extent possible, eliminate mealtime decisions, options, choices and uncertainty by deciding in advance what you are going to eat.

Getting your repeat day right will require some fun trial and error. (I still can't look at a Chipotle burrito bowl.) Your repeat day or Groundhog Day will need to be right for you in these four ways.

First, your calories must be right.

Being over by 200 calories every day will result in a gain of 20 pounds a year. I take in 200 calories by just smelling a bakery.

Second, your nutrition must be right.

Because this day is repeated, it is paramount that you get your macro-nutrients and micro-nutrients. Those nutrients will rebuild your cells and protect you from disease. You may want to talk with a nutritionist, or your internist, or a super healthy friend. Definitely Google power foods. This will be worth your time.

Third, get the satiety right.

CLUTCH

Don't live hungry or hangry. A calorie is not a calorie. Some foods produce strong cravings two hours after you eat them. (Due to blood sugar spikes and drops.) Some foods keep you satisfied for hours. And when you do get hungry, the hunger comes on low and slow. Again, this will require a bit of trial and error. Don't be surprised if you start eating more beans as they produce incredible satiety. Don't worry, the infamous gastro Jacuzzi side effect stage will…pass.

Finally, get the enjoyment right.

Enjoyment is key to sustainability. J. R. R. Tolkien said, "If more of us valued food and cheer and song above hoarded gold, it would be a merrier world."[61] Enjoying delicious food with your family and friends is part of the merry life. Keep working with your repeated day until you discover a wonderful, healthy, nutritious collection of food that you can celebrate and enjoy repeating.

A Routine for Eight Hours

Calorie intake is a 24/7 challenge. I can eat perfectly for 23 and a half hours per day and still find myself a contestant on The Biggest Loser. I've been known to eat like Cindy Crawford by day and Seabiscuit by night. Here is an excellent tool for cutting down the size of your daily challenge. Intermittent fasting.

Numerous studies have shown the following benefits of intermittent fasting:[62]

- decreased insulin levels
- increased levels of human growth hormone
- repair of cells
- loss of belly fat
- lowered risk of type 2 diabetes
- reduced inflammation
- reduced blood pressure
- improvement in cholesterol numbers
- cancer prevention
- improvement in brain health
- prevention of Alzheimer's
- lengthened lifespan

Did I hear you say "wow"? That is a wow list of benefits. Here is an easy change to your daily routine that will deliver those benefits to your brain and body. Fast for 16 hours a day. Eat for 8 hours each day. This is the most popular version of intermittent fasting. My goal is to eat lunch at 1:00 pm. My daily calorie intake, whenever possible, happens between 1:00 and 9:00.

Not only do I grab the benefits off the list above, I have found several other benefits. First, I have fully automated my eating (actually my not-eating) for 16 hours of my day. Once that is done, I only have to get my eating right for the remaining 8 hours. Getting it right for 8 hours is much easier. Second, my daily calorie allocation has not changed, I simply eat those calories closer together. This makes me feel like I'm getting much more food. Do a little research, talk with your doctor, and if you feel compelled, give intermittent fasting a go. I think you may like it.

A Routine of Celebration

I suggest that one day each week you throw your brilliantly crafted routine out the window. Enjoy one day of spontaneous culinary celebration. You have heard this day called a cheat day. I'm not fond of cheating. I'm quite fond of celebrating. I like to think that the slice of pie you eat for breakfast on your celebration day is as much a part of your health plan as the kale and spinach green drink on your repeat days. Here is why your celebration day is important.

Your celebration day is the pressure release value on your week of careful eating. It relieves any emotional strain that comes from making good choices all week. It is a weekly emotional reset button.

Your celebration day keeps you from feeling deprived. I was at a great restaurant one Thursday for lunch. The people I lunched with ordered apple pie. This was the Sistine Chapel ceiling of apple pie. Gorgeous. Fragrant. I wanted just one slice. Then I thought, instead of having one slice today, I'll come back Saturday, my special day, and eat an entire pie if I want. One guilty slice today vs. a whole, guiltless pie in 48 hours. Because I could do that I didn't feel deprived. I actually felt the opposite. I felt I'm on this really cool eating plan where I can eat pie every week and still be fit and healthy. Knowing this makes all the difference. It's the law of scarcity. We want what we can't have. The forbidden fruit. The forbidden fruit pie. With this approach, no food is disallowed, it's simply delayed.

Your celebration day also gives you a shot of additional calories each week to help you maintain your metabolism. The last thing we want is for our bodies to compensate for healthy eating by burning fewer calories.

I suggest only one rule for your celebration day. Even if I didn't mention this rule, you would discover it on your own in a couple of weeks. You will want to stop eating when full. It is not enjoyable to eat when you are not hungry. The first time I allowed myself a no-foods-barred day of celebration, I ate well past the point of enjoyment. That was not fun. Now I eat exactly what I want, but not all that much of it. Instead of having pie with dinner, I may have pie for dinner. Your day of celebration will teach you something that will help you the six other days. An apple when you are hungry tastes better than a donut when your belly is full.

Take a few minutes to write down your first draft of your eating routine. When you are ready, we'll move on to adding ceremony in the next chapter.

EXERCISE

Your Personal Power Ritual

• • •

The best part of any published diet plan is the plan itself. The plan tells you what to eat. You can do this for yourself. Yours will be much better. It will be tailor made just for you.

- How many calories does your body burn each day? (There are many apps to help you discover an exact number.)

- List a few healthy foods that you believe you can enjoy repeating.

- How might your nutritional Groundhog Day or week look?

CHAPTER *twenty-two*

CRAFT YOUR WEIGHT LOSS CEREMONY

"People who love to eat are always the best people."
- *Julia Child*

Here's our big idea in review.

You have found it difficult to change old "eating habits." Now you know why. Your old eating behavior is not a set of habits at all. It is a collection of powerful rituals. You didn't set out to craft eating rituals, nonetheless, that's exactly what you did. Your lifetime eating behavior is comprised of automated routines plus symbolic micro ceremonies. (Can you hear the clink of wine glasses?)

As you read the last chapter, you started scratching out your new eating routine. Your routine is practical. Your routine is left brain: logical, linear and mathematical. It describes the foods you will eat, the quantities, the calories, the timing. Well done you!

Other approaches to weight loss stop there. Atkins. South Beach. Paleo. Weight Watchers. Nutrisystem. Zone. They all provide left brain, practical eating routines. You know what the right brain adds. Imagination. Inspiration. Excitement. Positive emotions. Art. Creativity. Ceremony will make your new routine enjoyable.

A Ceremony to Enjoy

Psychological scientist Kathleen Vohs of the Carlson School of Management at the University of Minnesota noticed something about her morning espresso. "Whenever I order an espresso, I take a sugar packet and shake it, open the packet and pour a teeny bit of sugar in, and then taste," Vohs observes. "It's never enough sugar, so I then pour about half of the packet in."[63] She knows the teeny bit of sugar won't be enough. Time could be saved by skipping her teeny bit tasting.

This espresso observation inspired Vohs to lead extensive studies on how repeated ceremonies might enhance our enjoyment of various foods. Vohs first experimented with chocolate bars. Half of the participants were given detailed ritual instructions to follow. The other participants were instructed to simply relax for a bit and then eat the chocolate bar any way they wanted. The participants were then asked to write down how much they would pay for this chocolate bar. Those who had performed the ritual believed the chocolate to be of higher quality and therefore more valuable.[64]

Vohs next experiment showed that, "random movements don't produce a more enjoyable eating experience. Only repeated, episodic, and fixed behaviors seem to change our perception of the food."[65]

Vohs also discovered the value of ritual delay. A brief delay between ritual and consumption increased the positive effect of ritual.[66]

Finally, Vohs confirmed what others have observed, rituals reward active participation. Watching someone perform a food ceremony is not as beneficial as your participation in the ritual ceremony. By the way, in case you were wondering, Vohs did not always study delicious chocolate. She found that what was true of chocolate was also true of carrots.[67]

The ceremony you are about to craft may strike you as small and mundane. You may ask, is it really important? Is it worth the effort? Kathleen Vohs wants you to know, it is.

A Ceremony that is Unique

The purpose of your food ceremony is to elevate consciousness. It is symbolic behavior performed to focus and inspire. One way to go about crafting such a ceremony is to simply do something unique and unusual. Something that other people don't naturally do. Make it original and distinctive. Like the secret handshake for a club of one. Like Kathleen Vohs tiny espresso tasting.

Here are a few small and mundane prompts to get you thinking. You might say special words or a unique blessing before your meal. You could eat your meal in an unusual location like a patio, basement, park or garage. You could eat sitting on the hood of your car outside a Gold's Gym or yoga studio as fit people come and go. You can have a ceramic plate custom made with Ryan Gosling on it. If you eat with your family, you could have a special conversation. You could listen to TED Talks, podcasts or special music as you eat. You could eat with Rolex precision. Set start time. Set midpoint. Set time of final bite.

One summer I crafted a Washington Nationals baseball radio broadcast dinner ceremony. Most of the games started at 7:05 so my dinner started at 7:05. I ate and listened outside in a favorite Adirondack chair. To make it all the more unusual, I decided to do this regardless of the weather. It soon became quite fun. I found myself symbolically aligned with the challenges and goals of Bryce Harper, Stephen Strasburg, Max Scherzer, Ryan Zimmerman and Jayson Werth. Baseball is a daily grind. Regular season goes through the end of September. Playoffs go through the end of October. The Nationals had a baseball goal out in front of them. I had a health and fitness goal. My ceremony transformed a diet into a grand adventure.

A Ceremony that is Evocative

The other way to go about crafting your ceremony is to find an evocative element in your own story. Some element you lift from the pages of your unabridged autobiography. An evocative element reminds you of something important, significant or powerful. An evocative ceremony somehow encourages, inspires, motivates or strengthens you.

To find something evocative, you may need to take a mental journey home. Think about life when you were growing up. What was it like when you were five? Who was there at mealtime?

CLUTCH

Where did you sit? Where did you eat? Was dinner family style or did mom fill your plates? Did you hold hands and pray or did everybody dig in boarding house style? Was there too much food or not enough? Was the table a happy place or not? What was it like at age 10 or 15? Pretty much the same or had things changed? You may want to recreate one or two of your family's mealtime ceremonies. You may want to do something exactly the opposite.

Another evocative approach is to zoom in at mealtime on the brand new healthy you of your dreams. Vividly imagine the possibilities. Think of some way that goal can be incorporated in a mealtime ceremony.

One last note of encouragement. Because of the way we have been programmed to think about weight management, you will be tempted to invest 95% of your effort on your eating routine leaving only 5% for your ceremony. Pro tip: With any ritual, the secret sauce is always the ceremony.

EXERCISE

Your Personal Power Ritual

• • •

This final exercise of Clutch may be the most fun. You may want to save this exercise for your 100 minutes of genius. Extra points for coming up with a crazier idea than Ryan Gosling's face on a plate.

Brainstorm ideas about possible evocative food ceremonies. What would take you back?

Consider unique approaches to eating your meals. You only need a couple unique elements. Consider all possibilities. When. Where. How. Clothing. Music. Beverage. Go beyond those and create something new and fun.

CHAPTER *twenty-three*

YOU CAN RISE TO THE OCCASION

"Dream as if you'll live forever.
Live as if you'll die today."
- *James Dean*

My favorite book title of all time is by Kathryn Lindskoog. It's called *Creative Writing: For People Who Can't Not Write*. I'm one of those people.

Thirty-five years ago, a few brief words by Dr. Tony Campolo drew my attention to Durkheim's ground-breaking work on the surprising power of rituals. After the better part of four decades of reading everything I could find on the topic and endless personal and group experiments with ritual theory, I arrived at a moment when I knew *Clutch* was the book I can't not write. *Clutch* was the story I can't not tell. *Clutch* was the secret I can't not share.

Tony Robbins insists rituals equal results. If you don't understand why Tony says that, I hope you will soon. I believe you will find power and focus for your big game and get a bonus. Effervescence.

I love the words of Mihaly Csikszentmihalyi in *Flow: The Psychology of Happiness*, "Of all the virtues we can learn, no trait is more useful, more essential for survival, and more likely to improve the quality of life than the ability to transform adversity into an enjoyable challenge."[68]

I pray *Clutch* helps you rise to the occasion while enjoying the challenge.

Grace & peace,
Mark

APPENDIX

RITUAL POWER FOR YOUR GROUPS

"Without frequent ritual and ceremony,
the symbolic ties that hold people together unravel."
- *Terrence Deal*

Welcome to your bonus chapter.

This chapter is my opportunity to say, *Oh, by the way, what you have learned about power rituals has another important application.* Groups. Let's think for a moment about *group power rituals.*

The Family Dinner Project at Harvard University is a research-based proponent of family dinners. According to the Family Dinner Project, research has shown the following benefits of family dinners:[69]

- Improved academic performance
- Decreased risk of substance abuse
- Decreased rates of obesity
- Decreased risk of teen pregnancy
- Increased self-esteem
- Decreased risk of depression
- Greater sense of resilience
- Decreased risk of developing eating disorders

Wow! Does that list strike you as unbelievable? It does sound like hyperbolic hoopla. A campaign rally of promises. It reminds me of an infomercial elixir promising to grow new hair on your head, remove rust from old cars, and can be served to your friends as a delicious and nutritious beverage.

The family dinner research was nothing new. It was the latest support for the research conducted more than 100 years ago by French anthropologist, Emile Durkheim. Durkheim found that any group – armies, sports teams, business groups, church groups, families – with a high commitment to positive rituals were stronger in three ways. First, they had **greater solidarity**. They enjoyed wearing the team colors, flying the team flag, telling people they were part of the team. Second, they **shared values and dreams**. Third, each group member had **greater inner strength**. Greater resilience. Greater optimism. Each member dealt better with adversity. They fell down. They bounced back up.[70]

CLUTCH

Business Groups & Business Growth

Dr. W. Edwards Deming was considered the father of Japanese post-war industrialization and guru of quality controls in manufacturing. He is known for his 14 points for leaders. At the end of his illustrious career, Deming reduced his fourteen points and all his work into one key idea. The key to consistently producing any quality product is one thing. Leaders of people must activate the human spirit.[71] Group power rituals help do that.

> *"The human spirit is summoned most majestically in ritual and ceremony."*[72]

Terrence Deal and Allan Kennedy wrote a landmark book in 1982 entitled *Corporate Cultures: the Rites and Rituals of Corporate Life*. It grew out of a Stanford study of 80 of America's most successful companies. They were among the first to peer through spreadsheets, balance sheets and EBITDA earnings growth to see the tribal cultures producing that growth. They were among the first to conclude that strong, distinctive, ritualized business cultures were behind many of the great growth stories.[73]

John Kotter and James Haskett in *Corporate Culture and Performance* write about ritualized culture companies. According to their research, companies with highly ritualized cultures saw revenues increase by 682% versus 166% over the period of their study.[74]

Terrence Deal in a book called *Corporate Celebration* writes "Without frequent ritual and ceremony, the symbolic ties that hold people together unravel; people split apart from each other, severing emotional ties with the company and losing their common hope, faith and vision. As a result the company loses its competitive edge, delivers a lackluster performance, and posts a dismal financial return."[75]

To help you think about where you might use a group power ritual, let me introduce four common types. These four are not meant to be a complete list. But hopefully, they will get you started.

The Social Ritual

The social ritual is the most common group power ritual. Its primary purpose is to bring people together for fun and celebration. The corporate holiday party. The family movie night. The neighborhood summer picnic. Make sure you have routine, ceremony and repetition. These events, done well, break down barriers and open up communication, understanding and trust. Great leaders understand that positive, repeated social events help to create a powerful culture.

The Victory Ritual

The victory ritual can recognize individual heroes or the accomplishments in a family, business or on a team. They are the Olympic medal ceremony of groups. One of my favorites is from the heyday of Intel. For a period of time the great champions were honored with a box of M&M's. M&M's came to be the Oscar statue of Intel.

CLUTCH

The Loss Ritual

Perhaps the most powerful ritual for any group is the ritual enacted in a time of loss. More raw power is present in a circle of loss than in a circle of celebration. There is a greater need for ritual after a setback than after a victory. That's why the most ritualized event in every culture is the funeral.

In a business environment the loss may be the loss of a sale to the competition. A big client leaves. A key employee exits. The economy turns south. Too many business setbacks are met with silence. People hide. Shut their doors. Crawl under their desks. People hang their heads and leave by the back stairs. Business setbacks are huge opportunities to make the team stronger. The loss ritual could be the team gathering at a special restaurant for a postmortem meal. The team could always huddle up in a conference room with a special food or beverage for 30 minutes of reflection. The team could gather for the retelling of a story or the reciting of a creed and mission statement. The most important thing is to do something. The second most important thing is doing the same unique thing over and over.

A Navy SEALs loss ritual is explained in this blog post by Joe Holleman, retired USN Chief Petty Officer.

> "Navy SEALs don't leave flowers. SEALs are a brotherhood. These are men who put their lives in the hands of their team mates day in and day out in situations most people don't want to imagine. Pounding that Trident into the casket of a fallen brother means a piece of all of his team mates will

always be with him. That Trident is not something taken lightly, those guys go through hell to earn them and they don't just flippantly pass them out. For a SEAL to remove his Trident and pay tribute with it to a fallen brother is the ultimate respect for someone who gave their absolute all."[76]

The Value Ritual

Ritz-Carlton famously enacts a value ritual. A Ritz-Carlton senior executive told me a few stories from their legendary WOW meeting. The WOW meeting reinforces the Ritz-Carlton brand value of legendary customer service.

Every morning, people worldwide gather in a stand-up circle for the WOW story. It is the telling of one simple story of a Ritz-Carlton employee who did some amazingly gracious thing for a guest. As a result of this value ritual, every future guest of Ritz-Carlton is more likely to be wowed.

You Can Do This

Even with only this brief introduction to group power rituals, I believe you are ready to give it a go. Family is a perfect place to start. Make sure you add ceremony. I think you'll soon say, "wow."

REFERENCES

[1] Benedetto De Martino, Vikram S. Chib, John P. O'Doherty, and Shinsuke Shimojo, "Neural Mechanisms Underlying Paradoxical Performance for Monetary Incentives Are Driven by Loss Aversion," *Neuron* 74, no. 3 (May 10, 2012): 582-94, doi:10.1016/j.neuron.2012.02.038.

[2] Bill Russell and Taylor Branch, *Second wind: the memoirs of an opinionated man* (New York: Ballantine Books, 1980), 177.

[3] Lance P. Hickey, PhD, "'Flow' Experiences: The Secret to Ultimate Happiness?" *HuffPost*, January 22, 2011, accessed August 20, 2017, http://www.huffingtonpost.com/lance-p-hickey-phd/flow-experiences-happiness_b_811682.html.

[4] Andrew Cooper, "In the Zone: The Zen of Sports," *Lion's Roar*, March 1, 1995, accessed August 31, 2017, https://www.lionsroar.com/in-the-zone-the-zen-of-sports/.

[5] James E. Loehr, *Mental toughness training for sports: achieving athletic excellence* (Lexington, Massachusetts: Stephen Greene Press, Inc., 1986), 22.

[6] Mihaly Csikszentmihalyi, *Flow: The psychology of optimal experience* (New York: Harper Row, 2009).

[7] Ibid.

[8] Steven Kotler, *The rise of superman: decoding the science of ultimate human performance* (London: Quercus, 2015), viii.

[9] Csikszentmihalyi.

[10] Michaéla C. Schippers and Paul A. M. Van Lange, "The Psychological Benefits of Superstitious Rituals in Top Sport: A Study Among Top Sportspersons," *Journal of Applied Social Psychology* 36, no. 10 (September 15, 2006): 2532-553, doi:10.1111/j.0021-9029.2006.00116.x.

[11] DeAnn L. Lobmeyer and Edward A. Wasserman, "Preliminaries to free throw shooting: superstitious behavior?" *Journal of Sport Behavior* (June 1986): 70-78.

[12] Judy L. Van Raalte, Britton W. Brewer, Carol J. Nemeroff, and Darwyn E. Linder, "Chance orientation and superstitious behavior on the putting green," *Journal of Sport Behavior* (March 1991): 41-50.

[13] Michael Norton and Francesca Gino, "Rituals alleviate grieving for loved ones, lovers, and lotteries," *Journal of Experimental Psychology: General* 143, no. 1 (February 2014): 266-72, doi:10.1037/a0031772.

[14] Ibid.

[15] "Cal Fussman-The Master Storyteller Returns," Interview. *The Tim Ferriss Show*(audio blog), August 31, 2016, accessed August 30, 2017, https://tim.blog/2016/08/31/cal-fussman-the-master-storyteller-returns/.

[16] Norton, "Rituals alleviate grieving", 269.

[17] Emile Durkheim and Joseph Ward Swain, *The elementary forms of religious life* (Mansfield Centre, CT: Martino Publishing, 2012).

[18] Lisa Rogak, *Haunted heart: the life and times of Stephen King* (New York: Thomas Dunne Books/St. Martin's Griffin, 2010).

[19] Annie Dillard, *The writing life* (New York: Harper Perennial, 2013).

[20] Rob Harms, "Enter Sound Man: An Insider's Look at Baseball's Walk-Up Music," New York Times, July 31, 2015, accessed October 23, 2017, https://www.nytimes.com/2015/08/02/sports/baseball/enter-sound-man-an-insiders-look-at-baseballs-walk-up-music.html.

[21] Carmen Nobel, "The Power of Rituals in Life, Death, and Business." *HBS Working Knowledge*, June 03, 2013 accessed October 11, 2017, http://hbswk.hbs.edu/item/the-power-of-rituals-in-life-death-and-business.

[22] Kathleen Vohs, Yajin Wang, Francesca Gino, and Michael I. Norton, "Rituals Enhance Consumption," *Psychological Science* 24, no. 9 (September 13, 2013): 1714-721, doi:10.1037/e509992015-121.

CLUTCH

[23] Shawn Achor, *The happiness advantage: the seven principles of positive psychology that fuel success and performance at work* (New York: Broadway Books, 2010), 37.

[24] Alan Ley, "ITU Athlete Routines, Rituals, & Performance Strategies." *The Sport Journal* (March 27, 2015), accessed September 06, 2017, http://thesportjournal.org/article/itu-athlete-routines-rituals-performance-strategies.

[25] Norton, "Rituals alleviate grieving".

[26] Ibid., 266.

[27] Ibid., 269-271.

[28] Michael Lewis, "Michael Lewis: Obama's Way," *The Hive*, January 29, 2015, accessed September 06, 2017, https://www.vanityfair.com/news/2012/10/michael-lewis-profile-barack-obama.

[29] William James, *Psychology: the briefer course* (Mineola, NY: Dover Publications, Inc., 2001).

[30] Ibid., 12.

[31] William James and Henry James, *The letters of William James: 2 vol. combined* (New York: Cosimo, 2008), 148.

[32] Roy F. Baumeister and John Tierney, *Willpower: rediscovering the greatest human strength* (New York: Penguin Books, 2012), 2.

[33] Kelly McGonigal, *The willpower instinct: how self-control works, why it matters, and what you can do to get more of it* (New York: Avery, 2011), 1.

[34] Ibid., 55.

[35] Mason Currey, *Daily rituals: how artists work* (New York: Alfred A. Knopf, 2013), kindle edition.

[36] Schippers, "The Psychological Benefits of Superstitious Rituals."

[37] Benjamin Mack, "Athlete rituals a theater of the bizarre," *DW.COM*, October 8, 2012, accessed September 06, 2017, http://www.dw.com/en/athlete-rituals-a-theater-of-the-bizarre/a-16150087.

[38] Ibid.

[39] J.N. Nielsen, "Take Comfort in Rituals," *Grand Strategy: The View from Oregon*, September 26, 2010, accessed September 06, 2017, https://geopolicraticus.wordpress.com/tag/starbucks.

[40] Tim Ferriss, "Podcast – The Tim Ferriss Show," *The Blog of Author Tim Ferriss*, accessed September 19, 2017, https://tim.blog/podcast/.

[41] Tony Robbins, "Tony Robbins Audiobook® Hour of Power," *YouTube*, May 11, 2017, accessed September 19, 2017, https://www.youtube.com/watch?v=TB4ZK8qmUrM.

[42] Ibid.

[43] Adam Siemiginowski, "Drawing Down the Vision." *Drawing Down the Vision, a practical guide to living and working creatively*, March 11, 2011, accessed September 19, 2017, http://drawingdownthevision.com/2011/03/.

[44] Currey, *Daily rituals*, Kindle edition.

[45] Tony Robbins, "Tony Robbins: 'Gratitude Is the Solution to Anger and Fear'," *Thrive Global*, November 29, 2016, accessed September 20, 2017, https://journal.thriveglobal.com/tony-robbins-gratitude-is-the-solution-to-anger-and-fear-c3fa819825c.

[46] Tom Ziglar, "The Gratitude Journey," *Ziglar Inc.*, March 30, 2017, accessed September 19, 2017, https://www.ziglar.com/articles/the-gratitude-journey/.

[47] Alex Korb, *The upward spiral: using neuroscience to reverse the course of depression, one small change at a time* (Oakland, CA: Harbinger Publications, Inc., 2015), Kindle edition.

[48] The Dixie Chicks, Not ready to make nice, Sony BMG Music Entertainment, 2006, MP3.

[49] Jim Prime and Bill Nowlin, *Tales from the Red Sox dugout* (USA: Sports Publishing, LLC, 2002), 13.

[50] Scott Cain, *Cleburne baseball: a railroader history* (Charleston, SC: The History Press, 2017), 114.

[51] Michael W. Kraus, Cassy Huang, and Dacher Keltner, "Tactile communication, cooperation, and performance: An ethological study of the NBA," *Emotion* 10, no. 5 (October 2010): 745-49, doi:10.1037/a0019382.

[52] Norton, "Rituals alleviate grieving".

[53] "Wes Adamson > Quotes," Wes Adamson Quotes (Author of Imagination by Moonlight), accessed October 23, 2017, https://www.goodreads.com/author/quotes/7303556.Wes_Adamson.

[54] "A quote by Dale Carnegie," Quote by Dale Carnegie: "People rarely succeed unless they have fun in w...", accessed October 23, 2017, https://www.goodreads.com/quotes/33781-people-rarely-succeed-unless-they-have-fun-in-what-they.

[55] Deborah Smith, "Psychologist Wins Nobel Prize: Daniel Kahneman is Honored for Bridging Economics and Psychology," *Monitor on Psychology* 33, no. 11 (December 2002): 22, doi:10.1037/e300122003-020.

[56] Daniel Kahneman and Amos Tversky, "Judgment under Uncertainty: Heuristics and Biases," *The Journal of the Operational Research Society* 34, no. 3 (1983): 254, doi:10.2307/2581328.

[57] Amanda Scherker, "9 Famous Geniuses Who Were Also Huge Coffee Addicts," *The Huffington Post*, June 02, 2014, accessed September 20, 2017, http://www.huffingtonpost.com/2014/06/02/famous-coffee-drinkers_n_5358495.html.

[58] Martin Seligman and John Tierney, "We Aren't Built to Live in the Moment," *New York Times*, May 19, 2017, accessed September 20, 2017, https://www.nytimes.com/2017/05/19/opinion/sunday/why-the-future-is-always-on-your-mind.html.

[59] Laird Hamilton, "A Diet You Can Live With," *Men's Journal*, August 16, 2013, accessed September 20, 2017, http://www.mensjournal.com/expert-advice/laird-hamilton-a-diet-you-can-live-with-20130816.

[60] Malcolm Gladwell, "The 10,000-hour rule," In *Outliers: the story of success* (New York: Back Bay Books, Little, Brown and Company, 2008).

[61] "The Hobbit Quotes by J.R.R. Tolkien." By J.R.R. Tolkien. Accessed October 23, 2017. https://www.goodreads.com/work/quotes/1540236-the-hobbit-or-there-and-back-again.

[62] Kris Gunnars, "10 Evidence-Based Health Benefits of Intermittent Fasting," *Healthline*, August 16, 2016, accessed September 21, 2017, http://www.healthline.com/nutrition/10-health-benefits-of-intermittent-fasting.

[63] "To Savor the Flavor, Perform a Short Ritual First," *Association for Psychological Science*, July 22, 2013, accessed September 21, 2017, http://www.psychologicalscience.org/news/releases/to-savor-the-flavor-perform-a-short-ritual-first.html.

[64] Ibid.

[65] Ibid.

[66] Ibid.

[67] Ibid.

[68] Mihaly Csikszentmihalyi, *Flow the psychology of happiness* (London: Rider, 1998), 200.

[69] "Benefits of Family Dinners," *The Family Dinner Project*, 2017, accessed October 10, 2017, https://thefamilydinnerproject.org/about-us/benefits-of-family-dinners.

[70] Durkheim, *The elementary forms of religious life*.

[71] Terrence E. Deal and M. K. Key, *Corporate celebration: play, purpose, and profit at work* (San Francisco: Berrett-Koehler, 1998), xi.

[72] Ibid.

[73] Terrence E. Deal and Allan A. Kennedy. *Corporate cultures: the rites and rituals of corporate life* (New York: Basic Books, 2002).

[74] Kotter, John P., and James L. Heskett. *Corporate culture and performance* (Simon and Schuster, 2008), 78.

[75] Deal, *Corporate celebration: play, purpose, and profit at work*, 11.

[76] Joe Holleman, "What is the significance of a fellow sailor pounding a Navy SEAL trident into a fallen sailor's casket, e.g., what is this tradition's origin, is it expected for a fellow sailor in attendance to do it, and do other branches also do it?" *Quora*, June 23, 2015, accessed October 10, 2017, https://www.quora.com/What-is-the-significance-of-a-fellow-sailor-pounding-a-Navy-SEAL-trident-into-a-fallen-sailors-casket-e-g-what-is-this-tradition%E2%80%99s-origin-is-it-expected-for-a-fellow-sailor-in-attendance-to-do-it-and-do-other-branches-also-do-it.

BIBLIOGRAPHY

Achor, Shawn. *The happiness advantage: the seven principles of positive psychology that fuel success and performance at work.* New York: Broadway Books, 2010.

Baumeister, Roy F., and John Tierney. *Willpower: rediscovering the greatest human strength.* New York: Penguin Books, 2012.

"Benefits of Family Dinners." *The Family Dinner Project.* 2017. Accessed October 10, 2017. https://thefamilydinnerproject.org/about-us/benefits-of-family-dinners.

Cain, Scott. *Cleburne baseball: a railroader history.* Charleston, SC: The History Press, 2017.

"Cal Fussman-The Master Storyteller Returns." Interview. *The Tim Ferriss Show*(audio blog). August 31, 2016. Accessed August 30, 2017. https://tim.blog/2016/08/31/cal-fussman-the-master-storyteller-returns.

Cooper, Andrew. "In the Zone: The Zen of Sports." *Lion's Roar.* March 1, 1995. Accessed August 31, 2017. https://www.lionsroar.com/in-the-zone-the-zen-of-sports.

Csikszentmihalyi, Mihaly. *Flow: the psychology of happiness.* London: Rider, 1998.

Csikszentmihalyi, Mihaly. *Flow: The psychology of optimal experience.* New York: Harper Row, 2009.

Currey, Mason. *Daily rituals: how artists work.* New York: Alfred A. Knopf, 2013. Kindle edition.

De Martino, Benedetto, Vikram S. Chib, John P. O'Doherty, and Shinsuke Shimojo. "Neural Mechanisms Underlying Paradoxical Performance for Monetary Incentives Are Driven by Loss Aversion." *Neuron* 74, no. 3 (May 10, 2012): 582-94. doi:10.1016/j.neuron.2012.02.038.

Deal, Terrence E., and Allan A. Kennedy. *Corporate cultures: the rites and rituals of corporate life*. New York: Basic Books, 2002.

Deal, Terrence E., and M. K. Key. *Corporate celebration: play, purpose, and profit at work*. San Francisco: Berrett-Koehler, 1998.

Dillard, Annie. *The writing life*. New York: Harper Perennial, 2013.

The Dixie Chicks. Not ready to make nice. Sony BMG Music Entertainment, 2006, MP3.

Durkheim, Emile, and Joseph Ward Swain. *The elementary forms of religious life*. Mansfield Centre, CT: Martino Publishing, 2012. (Original work published in 1912).

Ferriss, Tim. "Podcast – The Tim Ferriss Show." *The Blog of Author Tim Ferriss*. Accessed September 19, 2017. https://tim.blog/podcast/.

Gladwell, Malcolm. "The 10,000-hour rule." In *Outliers: the story of success*. New York: Back Bay Books, Little, Brown and Company, 2008.

Gunnars, Kris. "10 Evidence-Based Health Benefits of Intermittent Fasting." *Healthline*. August 16, 2016. Accessed September 21, 2017. http://www.healthline.com/nutrition/10-health-benefits-of-intermittent-fasting.

Hamilton, Laird. "A Diet You Can Live With." *Men's Journal*. August 16, 2013. Accessed September 20, 2017. http://www.mensjournal.com/expert-advice/laird-hamilton-a-diet-you-can-live-with-20130816.

Harms, Rob. "Enter Sound Man: An Insider's Look at Baseball's Walk-Up Music." *New York Times*. July 31, 2015. Accessed October 23, 2017. https://www.nytimes.com/2015/08/02/sports/baseball/enter-sound-man-an-insiders-look-at-baseballs-walk-up-music.html.

CLUTCH

Hickey, Lance P., Ph.D. "'Flow' Experiences: The Secret to Ultimate Happiness?" *HuffPost*. January 22, 2011. Accessed August 20, 2017. http://www.huffingtonpost.com/lance-p-hickey-phd/flow-experiences-happiness_b_811682.html.

"The Hobbit Quotes by J.R.R. Tolkien," *By J.R.R. Tolkien*, accessed October 23, 2017, https://www.goodreads.com/work/quotes/1540236-the-hobbit-or-there-and-back-again.

Holleman, Joe. "What is the significance of a fellow sailor pounding a Navy SEAL trident into a fallen sailor's casket, e.g., what is this tradition's origin, is it expected for a fellow sailor in attendance to do it, and do other branches also do it?" *Quora*. June 23, 2015. Accessed October 10, 2017. https://www.quora.com/What-is-the-significance-of-a-fellow-sailor-pounding-a-Navy-SEAL-trident-into-a-fallen-sailors-casket-e-g-what-is-this-tradition%E2%80%99s-origin-is-it-expected-for-a-fellow-sailor-in-attendance-to-do-it-and-do-other-branches-also-do-it.

James, William. *Psychology: the briefer course*. Mineola, NY: Dover Publications, Inc., 2001. First published in 1892 by Henry Holt and Company.

James, William, and Henry James. *The letters of William James: 2 vol. combined*. New York: Cosimo, 2008. First published in 1920 by the Atlantic Monthly Press.

Kidd, John, D. Kahneman, P. Slovic, and A. Tversky. "Judgment under Uncertainty: Heuristics and Biases." *The Journal of the Operational Research Society* 34, no. 3 (1983): 254. doi:10.2307/2581328.

Korb, Alex. *The upward spiral: using neuroscience to reverse the course of depression, one small change at a time*. Oakland, CA: Harbinger Publications, Inc., 2015. Kindle edition.

Kotler, Steven. *The rise of superman: decoding the science of ultimate human performance*. London: Quercus, 2015.

Kotter, John P., and James L. Heskett. *Corporate culture and performance*. Simon and Schuster, 2008.

Kraus, Michael W., Cassy Huang, and Dacher Keltner. "Tactile communication, cooperation, and performance: An ethological study of the NBA." *Emotion* 10, no. 5 (October 2010): 745-49. doi:10.1037/a0019382.

Lewis, Michael. "Michael Lewis: Obama's Way." *The Hive*. January 29, 2015. Accessed September 06, 2017. https://www.vanityfair.com/news/2012/10/michael-lewis-profile-barack-obama.

Ley, Alan. "ITU Athlete Routines, Rituals, & Performance Strategies." *The Sport Journal* (March 27, 2015). Accessed September 06, 2017. http://thesportjournal.org/article/itu-athlete-routines-rituals-performance-strategies/.

Lobmeyer, DeAnn L., and Edward A. Wasserman. "Preliminaries to free throw shooting: superstitious behavior?" *Journal of Sport Behavior* (June 1986): 70-78.

Loehr, James E. *Mental toughness training for sports: achieving athletic excellence*. Lexington, Massachusetts: Stephen Greene Press, Inc., 1986. First published in 1982 by Forum Publishing Company under the title *Athletic Excellence: Mental Toughness Training for Sports*.

Mack, Benjamin. "Athlete rituals a theater of the bizarre." *DW.COM*. October 8, 2012. Accessed September 06, 2017. http://www.dw.com/en/athlete-rituals-a-theater-of-the-bizarre/a-16150087.

McGonigal, Kelly. *The willpower instinct: how self-control works, why it matters, and what you can do to get more of it*. New York: Avery, 2011.

CLUTCH

Nielsen, J. N. "Take Comfort in Rituals." *Grand Strategy: The View from Oregon.* September 26, 2010. Accessed September 06, 2017. https://geopolicraticus.wordpress.com/tag/starbucks/.

Nobel, Carmen. "The Power of Rituals in Life, Death, and Business." *HBS Working Knowledge.* June 03, 2013. Accessed October 11, 2017. http://hbswk.hbs.edu/item/the-power-of-rituals-in-life-death-and-business.

Norton, Michael, and Francesca Gino. "Rituals alleviate grieving for loved ones, lovers, and lotteries." *Journal of Experimental Psychology: General* 143, no. 1 (February 2014): 266-72. doi:10.1037/a0031772.

Prime, Jim, and Bill Nowlin. *Tales from the Red Sox dugout.* USA: Sports Publishing, LLC, 2002.

"A quote by Dale Carnegie." *Quote by Dale Carnegie: "People rarely succeed unless they have fun in w...".* Accessed October 23, 2017. https://www.goodreads.com/quotes/33781-people-rarely-succeed-unless-they-have-fun-in-what-they.

Robbins, Tony. "Tony Robbins Audiobook® Hour of Power." *YouTube.* May 11, 2017. Accessed September 19, 2017. https://www.youtube.com/watch?v=TB4ZK8qmUrM.

Robbins, Tony. "Tony Robbins: 'Gratitude Is the Solution to Anger and Fear'." *Thrive Global.* November 29, 2016. Accessed September 20, 2017. https://journal.thriveglobal.com/tony-robbins-gratitude-is-the-solution-to-anger-and-fear-c3fa819825c.

Rogak, Lisa. *Haunted heart: the life and times of Stephen King.* New York: Thomas Dunne Books/St. Martin's Griffin, 2010.

Russell, Bill, and Taylor Branch. *Second wind: the memoirs of an opinionated man.* New York: Ballantine Books, 1980.

Scherker, Amanda. "9 Famous Geniuses Who Were Also Huge Coffee Addicts." *The Huffington Post*. June 02, 2014. Accessed September 20, 2017. http://www.huffingtonpost.com/2014/06/02/famous-coffee-drinkers_n_5358495.html.

Schippers, Michaéla C., and Paul A. M. Van Lange. "The Psychological Benefits of Superstitious Rituals in Top Sport: A Study Among Top Sportspersons." *Journal of Applied Social Psychology* 36, no. 10 (September 15, 2006): 2532-553. doi:10.1111/j.0021-9029.2006.00116.x.

Seligman, Martin, and John Tierney. "We Aren't Built to Live in the Moment." *New York Times*. May 19, 2017. Accessed September 20, 2017. https://www.nytimes.com/2017/05/19/opinion/sunday/why-the-future-is-always-on-your-mind.html.

Siemiginowski, Adam. "Drawing Down the Vision." *Drawing Down the Vision, a practical guide to living and working creatively*. March 11, 2011. Accessed September 19, 2017. http://drawingdownthevision.com/2011/03/.

Smith, Deborah. "Psychologist Wins Nobel Prize: Daniel Kahneman is Honored for Bridging Economics and Psychology." *Monitor on Psychology* 33, no. 11 (December 2002): 22. doi:10.1037/e300122003-020.

"To Savor the Flavor, Perform a Short Ritual First." *Association for Psychological Science*. July 22, 2013. Accessed September 21, 2017. http://www.psychologicalscience.org/news/releases/to-savor-the-flavor-perform-a-short-ritual-first.html.

Van Raalte, Judy L., Britton W. Brewer, Carol J. Nemeroff, and Darwyn E. Linder. "Chance orientation and superstitious behavior on the putting green." *Journal of Sport Behavior* (March 1991): 41-50.

Vohs, Kathleen, Yajin Wang, Francesca Gino, and Michael I. Norton. "Rituals Enhance Consumption." *Psychological Science* 24, no. 9 (September 13, 2013): 1714-721. doi:10.1037/e509992015-121.

"Wes Adamson > Quotes." *Wes Adamson Quotes (Author of Imagination by Moonlight)*. Accessed October 23, 2017. https://www.goodreads.com/author/quotes/7303556.Wes_Adamson.

Ziglar, Tom. "The Gratitude Journey." *Ziglar Inc*. March 30, 2017. Accessed September 19, 2017. https://www.ziglar.com/articles/the-gratitude-journey/.

Ritual Enthusiast.

Storyteller.

Sailor.

Dr. Mark Powell's interest in the power of personal rituals began with one throwaway line by a sociology professor: *Oh and, by the way, research shows the higher the level of rituals in a person's life, the stronger the person.* Those words prompted research, discoveries, speaking and *Clutch*.

Mark's favorite personal rituals involve black coffee and blue sailboats. He lives with his wife Annie and a Golden Retriever (whom he calls "dog") in Leesburg, Virginia.

drmarkpowell.com